"一带一路" 城市可持续发展报告
Belt and Road Sustainable Cities Development Series Reports

城市可持续发展

中欧的主要挑战与优秀案例

Sustainable Urban Development:

Challenges and Good Practices in Europe and China

中欧可持续发展报告课题组　著

By China–EU Sustainable Development Research Group

中国社会科学出版社

图书在版编目（CIP）数据

城市可持续发展：中欧的主要挑战与优秀案例：汉英对照／中欧可持续发展报告课题组著 . —北京：中国社会科学出版社，2019.4
（"一带一路"城市可持续发展报告）
ISBN 978 - 7 - 5203 - 4189 - 9

Ⅰ.①城…　Ⅱ.①中…　Ⅲ.①城市经济—经济可持续发展—国际合作—经济合作—研究报告—中国、欧洲—汉、英
Ⅳ.①F299.2②F299.5

中国版本图书馆 CIP 数据核字（2019）第 047190 号

出 版 人	赵剑英
责任编辑	王　衡
特约编辑	王玉静
责任校对	朱妍洁
责任印制	王　超

出　　版	中国社会科学出版社
社　　址	北京鼓楼西大街甲 158 号
邮　　编	100720
网　　址	http：//www.csspw.cn
发 行 部	010 - 84083685
门 市 部	010 - 84029450
经　　销	新华书店及其他书店

印刷装订	北京君升印刷有限公司
版　　次	2019 年 4 月第 1 版
印　　次	2019 年 4 月第 1 次印刷

开　　本	880×1230　1/32
印　　张	8.5
字　　数	181 千字
定　　价	68.00 元

凡购买中国社会科学出版社图书，如有质量问题请与本社营销中心联系调换
电话：010 - 84083683

中欧可持续发展报告课题组

中国城市和小城镇改革发展中心

吴程程　　刘　悦

朱沛琦　　冯　奎

冯　波　　魏劭琨

张津京

欧洲城市联合研究计划

Manfred HORVAT

Margit NOLL

Johannes RIEGLER

Magnus BRINK, JPI UE

Katarina SCHYLBERG

前　　言

　　不断涌现的新技术以及与之相适应的治理变革，正在全球范围内产生强烈冲击。城市作为人口与经济活动高度密集、人与自然高强度互动的地点，普遍面临从发展到可持续发展转型的挑战。建立从地方到全球不同层面强有力的合作伙伴关系，交流分享各种背景下成功的案例实践，将会极大促进全球城市的这一转型进程可持续城市服务和基础设施领域知识、技术和经验的交流与共创为解决城市规划、环境、健康、水务、交通、信息通讯技术、危害、韧性、减轻灾害风险和提高人民福祉等方面问题提供广阔的前景。

　　为此，欧洲城市联合研究计划（以下简称"欧洲城市计划"）和中国城市和小城镇改革发展中心（以下简称"中国城市中心"）于2016年开始合作，通过交流知识、建立战略层面对话，聚集中欧专家的专业知识。欧洲城市计划是欧洲挑战驱动型研究和创新倡议，共涉及20个国家。自2012年至今，已在可持续和宜居城市地区领域资助 70 多个项目，主要侧重"城市创新应用实验室"、试验科学与政策转化。中国城市中心是中华人民共和国国家发展和改革委员会的直属事业单位，主要从事城镇化和城市发展的政策研究和咨询。自 1998 年成立以来，中国城市中心一直为中国部委和地方政府提供政策研究和咨询服务并开展国际合作项目。鉴于欧洲城市计划和中国城市中心的职能和工作内容，二者通过知识交流、思想碰撞、对城市转型优秀案例的分析等方式为联合国可持续发展目标和《新城市议程》在欧洲与中国的落实一起贡献力量。

中国城市和小城镇改革　　　欧洲城市联合研究
发展中心主任、研究员　　　计划管理委员会主席
史育龙　　　　　　　　　马吉特·诺尔（Margit Noll）
　　　　　　　　　　　　　　　2019 年 4 月

目　　录

摘　　要

近年来，全球对于城市地区的认识发生了改变。过去，城市地区通常被描述为社会挑战（如污染、交通堵塞、健康风险等）于空间上集中呈现的某个地方，现在则被理解为经济社会活动集聚产生变革的地方。快速、规模空前的城市化尽管带来挑战，但可以主要理解为城市转型带来机会的过程。

一　可持续发展目标——为全球城市
可持续发展提供参考

从全球层面看，城市化带来的变革力量有利于应对社会挑战的观点在全球政策、议程和指南中均有所强调。在《2030 年可持续发展议程》中，联合国概括了影响人类和地球至关重要的领域的 17 个可持续发展目标，以激发未来 15

年的行动①。从该议程赋予城市地区的角色上看，城市地区对于实现可持续发展目标的重要性显而易见——"可持续发展目标 11：可持续城市和社区"完全侧重城市化，其余 16 个目标也都有涉及城市内容。所有 17 个目标及其分目标都明确指出城市可持续发展对于人类和地球的重要性，其中有 90 个指标（共 169 个）涉及城市地区。

"可持续发展目标 11"首次表达了在全球层面的政治、政策和实践中讨论可持续城市化和城市发展的必要性。联合国人居署随后发布了几乎由所有成员国签署的相关文件——《新城市议程》，阐释了城市化有助于构建可持续的未来、为全人类带来利益和机会的共同愿景。这标志着一个根本性变革，即确认可持续发展为应对城市挑战解决方案的组成部分。"可持续发展目标 11"和《新城市议程》的重要性取得全球共识，为实现可持续发展路径所涉及的目标和愿景提供了全球性参考框架。

上述愿景和实现路径体现了对城市化的理解从导致环境和社会问题的动态过程到产生变革性力量的过程的根本性演变②。

---

① United Nations, Transforming our World: The 2030 Agenda for Sustainable Development, 2015, p. 3.

② Foreword by Joan Clos: UN-Habitat, National Urban Policy: A Guiding Framework, 2015.

可持续发展转型方法多元化且涉及不同内容，包括一系列倡议、活动、项目、方法和利益攸关方等。为实现上述城市转型，城市政策、研究和创新所涉及的不同方法需要克服部门分割并整合不同的方法和技术①。同时，还需要理解其在何处可以增加转型潜力，在何处自相矛盾的战略、方法和执行会导致两难困境并可能妨碍转型力量的增强。

二　从国际交流中受益

实现全球城市转型需要建立从地方到全球不同层面强有力的合作伙伴关系。机构、城市、项目、倡议间的双边和多边伙伴关系可以提供更有效、更有针对性的能力建设国际支持。可持续城市服务和基础设施领域知识、技术和经验的交流与共创为解决城市规划、环境、健康、水务、交通、信息通信技术、危害、韧性方面的问题，以及减轻灾害风险和提高人民福祉等提供广阔的前景。

为此，欧洲城市联合研究计划（以下简称"欧洲城市计划"）和中国城市和小城镇改革发展中心（以下简称"中国城

---

① Bylund, J., Connecting the Dots by Obstacles? Friction and Traction Ahead for the SRIA Urban Transitions Pathway, 2016.

市中心")于 2016 年开始合作,旨在交流知识、建立战略层面对话、聚集中欧专家的专业知识。欧洲城市计划是挑战驱动型研究和创新倡议。自 2012 年至今,已在可持续和宜居城市地区领域资助 70 多个项目,主要侧重"城市创新应用实验室"、试验和科学—政策转化。中国城市中心是中华人民共和国国家发展和改革委员会的直属事业单位,主要从事城市化和城市发展的政策研究和咨询。自 1998 年成立以来,中国城市中心一直为中国部委和地方政府提供政策研究和咨询服务并开展国际合作项目。鉴于欧洲城市计划和中国城市中心的职能和工作内容,二者通过交流知识、激发讨论、提高对城市转型优秀案例的认识等方式为可持续发展目标和《新城市议程》在欧洲和中国的本地化和落实一起贡献力量。

三 创新方法与中欧案例

报告选取了五个涉及城市可持续发展的专题领域。每个专题领域都提供了由欧洲城市计划资助的欧洲案例和中国的创新项目/城市案例,展示优秀案例并强调运用创新方法对实现可持续发展目标的积极作用。以下是五个专题领域的案例概要。

1. 可持续城市规划和城市更新

以人为本的城市规划和对已有住宅区的节能及提高生活质

量的改造是城市可持续发展非常重要的内容。报告中的欧洲
SubUrbanLab 案例展示了城市创新应用实验室的共同设计和参
与式规划如何在物质和社会层面提升弱势社区。许多中国城市
地区的超大街区降低了可步行性。中国四川省南充市的大规模
城市更新项目阐释了如何通过可持续城市规划和城市更新将微
尺度开发植入已有的大尺度建设，从而提高可步行性，增强城
市地区的可持续性和宜居性。

2. 能效与低碳发展

城市地区在减少温室气体排放和提高能效方面具有巨大潜
力，对减缓气候变化可以产生积极影响。这不仅需要可再生能
源技术或创新能源管理，而且需要改变能源消费行为。报告中
的欧洲案例 me^2 项目旨在创建一个提高市民对能源消费认知的
社区平台，探索通过改变能源消费行为实现提高能效的方法。
me^2 概念通过了阿姆斯特丹（荷兰）和里斯本（葡萄牙）创
新应用实验室的测试。在中国，低碳发展在战略和城市层面推
行。中国多个部委通过发布生态城市政策和标准、启动试点城
市项目推动城市可持续发展。目前已有许多城市开始试点项
目，努力实现低碳发展。其中，最成功的案例之一——杭州
市，制定了宏伟的低碳发展计划，意在成为低碳城市和全国可
持续发展城市典范。

3. 交通出行

全世界都在努力改善交通出行系统，旨在为全人类提供安全的公共场所、商品、服务和经济机会的同时减少因交通出行产生的环境足迹。关于如何处理交通出行问题对其他经济（社会）、环境问题以及城市人口的生活质量和福祉问题产生的重要影响，报告提供了应用多模式出行系统和新的出行服务解决通勤和交通堵塞问题的案例。报告中的欧洲案例 Smart Commuting 项目分析了 3 个国家通勤者的出行行为，从而确定新出行服务的需求和潜力。该项目的成果不仅被政府采用而且转化为交通公司的商业解决方案。中国上海案例阐释了不同的智慧出行服务如何加强以公交、汽车、火车和自行车为主的多模式交通出行系统。通过一个综合的应用，不同交通出行模式的信息得以整合，门到门出行计划可以以多模式出行方式实现。

4. 共享经济

随着数字技术的发展和城市人口趋向于共享而非拥有的消费习惯，共享经济已成为现实。共享经济具有挑战固有消费模式的潜力，共享服务正从社会、环境和经济方面影响城市生活。在中国和欧洲，新的共享计划正在极大地影响城市生活和消费模式，并具有对城市可持续发展产生积极影响的潜力。报告中的欧洲案例 E4 - share 项目开发了灵活、高效、具有经济活力的汽车共享系统模型。该项目以维也纳城市为案例，在对比不同汽车共享模型、确定用户激励、回顾支持性政策框架的基础上开发此汽车共享系统模型。在中国，近年来共享经济迅猛发展。作为共享经济的一部分，杭州市于 2008 年首次推出公共自行车系统，在全市范围内提供与已有共同交通的无缝衔接，以缓解交通堵塞和环境问题。自 2015 年以来，随着创新技术的发展以及新共享机制和商业模式的出现，无桩共享单车在中国蓬勃发展。目前，共享单车与解决"最后一公里"、减少对汽车的依赖和温室气体排放等问题都具有密切联系。

5. 智慧城市治理

更有效地设计和实施城市可持续发展战略需要新的由公共和私营部门利益攸关方参与的合作治理。有利的技术、大数据和实时响应为创新和智慧城市治理和管理提供了新路径。当下，城市决策所需的多种信息来源容易获得，只是需要合适的工具和方法对信息进行整合和合成。报告中的欧洲案例 Urban-Data2Decide 项目处理来自社交媒体和开放数据的数据组，开发城市治理决策支持系统。数字技术和社交媒体同时支持参与式城市规划和治理。另一个欧洲案例 Incubators for Public Space 项目将新技术植入参与式规划过程，使所有利益攸关方都有机会为城市规划做贡献。该项目在伦敦、布鲁塞尔和都灵三个城市设有城市创新应用实验室。在中国，随着先进的信息和网络技术的应用，智慧城市治理体制创新在过去几年取得了突破性进展。"互联网＋"使城市治理和管理模式发生深刻变革。用更智慧的方式管理人口、检测城市道路网络和智能应急响应系统是智慧政府治理的三个典型例子。山东威海市智慧城市治理案例旨在通过体制改革和社会技术创新加强电子治理，从而加强政府治理能力、提高公共服务提供效率、改善民生。

四　结论

报告的结论部分通过分析中欧优秀案例间的异同，为中欧在城市可持续发展领域可能的合作内容和方式提供建议。报告仅筛选了部分欧洲优秀案例，而非全部。所选案例在某种程度上反映了欧洲城市计划在该领域资助的典型案例和中国城市可持续发展（包括试点城市、项目等）的总体情况。

中欧在城市可持续发展上具有相似之处，很大程度上是因为双方城市面临共同的挑战。差异之处，总体来说，主要是由于双方不同的城市化水平、经济社会发展阶段以及城市治理和城市可持续发展方式造成的。以下两点主要差异基于报告中的案例分析得出。

第一，不同规模和推广方式。总体来说，欧洲的优秀案例多偏向项目规模，更侧重测试理论框架、方法和创新技术，推广已经测试和检验的示范项目。中方的案例则更倾向于城市规模，更侧重在试点城市执行相关项目，然后选取更多的试点城市进行推广。

第二，不同的公众参与方式。中欧城市的公众参与方式有所不同。合作和共创式参与方式在欧洲案例中比在中国案例中运用更多。这可能是因为中国城市更多地采用自上而下的治理方式，欧洲的城市则更多地采用自上而下和自下而上相结合的治理方式。

除了反映规模和城市治理方式不同之外，报告中的案例也非常好地展示了城市转型需要综合性方法以及需要不同利益攸关方的参与。以下三点是原则上推动城市可持续发展的主要因素：（1）新技术解决方案或帮助解决具体城市挑战的社会创新；（2）利用上述新技术和社会机会创建城市转型框架的新治理模式和治理能力；（3）通过早期参与城市规划和发展过程，动员市民建立对新方法和解决方案的认知、改变行为、支持新解决方案的运用。

由此可见，实现城市可持续发展需要不同层面的所有利益攸关方（包括城市、企业、大学、研究机构和金融机构）的参与和努力，需要研究和创新的大力支持。在地方或城市层面处理这一复杂且带有实验性的情境（通过试点项目或者创新应用实验室）有助于解决城市面临的具体挑战，使所有利益攸关方都有机会参与合作、共创城市发展行动方案。参与过程中所产生的证据可以总结成优秀案例，结论可以在新政策、合作伙伴关系和商业模式上进一步应用。报告提供的案例强调了应用多个利益攸关方方法的潜力，为双方项目执行者间的进一步交流提供了有益参考。

鉴于中欧双方存在上述差异，也许值得在更好地了解地方性知识和需求的基础上探索对方市场。总体来看，欧方可能可以与中国的主要利益攸关方合作，通过分享已经测试和检验的示范项目为中国城市提供城市可持续发展框架和相关领域（如开放数据和城市创新应用实验室）的经验。中方具有广阔的市场和有利的创新环境，同时可能与欧方的主要利益攸关方合作，为欧洲城市提供信息网络技术和硬件基础设置。

此外，或许需要建立合作伙伴关系，动员和整合中欧双方主要利益攸关方资源。鉴于前文所述中国城市中心和欧洲城市计划的职能和工作内容，二者或许可以在中方和欧方发挥协调作用整合上述资源。合作方式建议包括但不限于以下内容：开展合作项目——邀请中欧主要利益攸关方参与，中欧城市作为试点和观察城市；组织各项活动——邀请中欧专家和主要利益攸关方参与，更好地了解地方性知识、交换可能可以转化、适应其他地方性情境的想法和经验。

第一章 导言

一 背景

近年来，全球对于城市地区的认识已发生改变。城市地区通常被描述为社会难题（如污染、交通堵塞、健康风险等）集中涌现的地方，而现在社会经济活动的聚集则被视为转型变革的一种资产。

其中，城市化是这种转型变革的重要推动力。2014年，全球54%的人口生活在城市地区，到2050年这个数字估计约为67%[①]。联合国估计，到2050年，全球城市人口将会从

---

① World Urbanisation Prospects—United Nations Department of Economic and Social Affairs, Population Division, 2014; J. Clos, "A 21st Century Vision for Urbanisation", OECD Development Matters, 8 June 2016.

2011 年的 36 亿增加至 53 亿[1]。由此成为人类居住史上最具实质性的转变。

　　城市化进程和模式以及发达国家和发展中国家之间的城市化水平存在差异[2]。在发达国家，大城市的人口将会减少，而中小城市的人口将会增多，从而出现一种平衡过程。发展中国家的特点是大城市正在吸引更多的人口，"最大限度地发挥积极的外部效应、尽量减少负面影响"[3]，由此构成了各国政府和市政当局的一项挑战。在发展中国家，城市化已成为一种持续存在的重要现象；根据预测，未来90%以上的城市增长都将出现在发展中国家[4]。随着农村人口不断流入城市，寻找机会提高自己和家庭的生活质量，预计到 2050 年全球 80% 以上

　　① O. Courtard, G. Finnveden, S. Kabitsch, R. Kitchin, R. Matos, P. Nijkamp, C. Pronello, D. Robinson, Urban Megatrends: Towards a European Research Agenda: A Report by the Scientific Advisory Board of the Joint Programming Initiative Urban Europe, 2014, p. 3; World Urbanisation Prospects—United Nations Department of Economic and Social Affairs, Population Division, 2014.

　　② Urban Europe—Statistics on Cities, Towns and Suburbs, Statistical Books, Eurostat, 2016, p. 8.

　　③ UN-Habitat, The Economic Role of Cities, United Nations Settlements Programme, Nairobi, 2011, p. 41.

　　④ Q. Z. Zhang:《世界城市化的趋势、承诺和挑战》,《国际城乡居住杂志》2016 年第 54 期; O. Courtard, G. Finnveden, S. Kabitsch, R. Kitchin, R. Matos, P. Nijkamp, C. Pronello, D. Robinson, Urban Megatrends: Towards a European Research Agenda: A Report by the Scientific Advisory Board of the Joint Programming Initiative Urban Europe, 2014, p. 3。

的城市人口都出现在发展中国家①。

如图 1 和图 2 所示，各大洲、地区和国家之间也出现了极大差异。在欧洲和北美，城市化与 19 世纪和 20 世纪上半叶的工业化密切相关②；之后这个过程出现放缓，因为郊区化导致

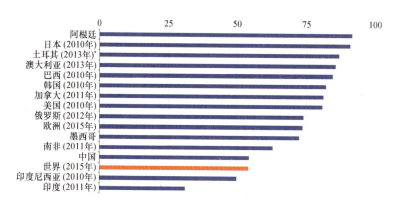

图 1　2014 年城市人口占比（城市居民百分比，%）

注：①联合国数据以国家定义为基础，因此本报告中的欧盟统计局数据可能与其他地方存在差异。②＊：估计值。

资料来源：《欧洲城市——城市、城镇和郊区统计数据》，2016 年，第 8 页。

---

① O. Courtard，G. Finnveden，S. Kabitsch，R. Kitchin，R. Matos，P. Nijkamp，C. Pronello，D. Robinson，Urban Megatrends：Towards a European Research Agenda；A Report by the Scientific Advisory Board of the Joint Programming Initiative Urban Europe，2014，p. 3.

② Q. Z. Zhang：《世界城市化的趋势、承诺和挑战》，《国际城乡居住杂志》2016 年第 54 期。

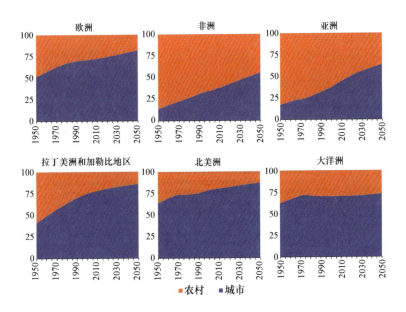

图 2　1950—2050 年世界城乡人口估计和预测数值

注：联合国数据以国家定义为基础，因此本报告中的欧盟统计局数据可能与其他地方存在差异。

资料来源：《世界城市化前景——联合国经济和社会事务部人口司》，2014 年。

了城市地区人口减少。居住郊区化存在不同的原因或驱动因素，比如住房成本更低，私家车数量增多，公共交通的发展缩短了城市中心与周边地区的通行时间，更惬意、更宜居的绿色环境，空气清新、环境宁静、可亲近大自然，可提供其他就业机会，与城市中心相比更加安全，以及人口结构变化。

　　根据最新数据①，目前已有 31 个城市的人口达到或超过
1000 万，其中亚洲 17 个，拉丁美洲 5 个，欧洲 4 个，非洲 3
个，北美洲 2 个。中国共有 6 个城市人口超过 1000 万，印度
有 5 个，巴西和日本各有 2 个，其他 16 个国家各有一个。到
2030 年，全球人口达到或超过 1000 万的特大城市数量将会增
至 41 个②。如此快速和规模空前的城市化以及世界人口向大
城市或特大城市集中虽然产生了持续挑战，但也为促进城市转
型提供了机会。

　　比如，大量农村人口在快速城市化的过程中涌入城市，导
致城市群不断增大，这在提供竞争优势和改善生活机会的同时
也给城市地区带来了巨大挑战。城市化与城市地区社会经济发
展之间的关系非常复杂。因此，为实现城市的可持续发展，需
重新评估城市发展方面的众多先决条件，比如就业机会、基础
设施、公共服务以及二氧化碳排放、气候变化、水资源、生物
多样性、社会包容性和人类健康等方面可能的影响③。

---

　　① 2018 世界城市人口，参见 http：//worldpopulationreview. com/world-cities。

　　② World Urbanisation Prospects，United Nations Department of Economic and Social Affairs，Population Division，2014，p. 1.

　　③ UN-Habitat，The Economic Role of Cities. United Nations Human Settlements
Programme，Nairobi，2011；M. Chen，H. Zhang，W. Liu，W. Zhang，"The Global Pat-
tern of Urbanization and Economic Growth：Evidence from the Last Three Decades"，
PLOS ONE，2014，9，8，p. 14.

可持续城市化并不存在一种普遍认同的定义。然而，为了能看到可持续性整体状况所需的不同视角，了解相关定义非常有用。实现可持续城市化需要多管齐下，采用综合式和交互式方法解决水、空气、土壤、能源、食品、交通、土地、生物多样性、化工、建筑、气候变化（适应气候变化和减缓气候变化）等经济发展和社会变革带来问题，而不是各自为战的"筒仓思维"①。

本报告采用了国际地方政府环境行动理事会（地方政府可持续发展协会）2016 年的定义："可持续城市致力于为现有人口提供环境友好、经济健康和富有韧性的栖息地，同时又不损害后代的发展能力。"②

二　城市可持续发展的全球趋势、机遇和挑战

欧洲城市计划的科学咨询委员会在 2014 年的报告③中指

---

① 城市中心的扩散、它们对世界环境的影响以及全球环境基金的潜在作用。科学和技术咨询小组：《可持续城市化政策简报》，2014 年，第 4 页。

② http://www.iclei.org/activities/agendas/sustainable-city.html.

③ O. Courtard, G. Finnveden, S. Kabitsch, R. Kitchin, R. Matos, P. Nijkamp, C. Pronello, D. Robinson, Urban Megatrends: Towards a European Research Agenda: A Report by the Scientific Advisory Board of the Joint Programming Initiative Urban Europe, 2014.

出了一些全球趋势。

国际贸易、跨国公司的创建、出口导向的增加、世界贸易组织等发展机构以及贸易和投资便利化协议构成了全球化经济的要素。信息通信技术和交通运输行业的发展为全球互动与合作的急剧增多提供了支持。各种经济关系形成了不同类型的全球连通性。经济全球化在过去和现在都是城市化的关键驱动力，城市和城市群是生产和消费的中心区，吸引来了拥有不同能力、专长和技能的人们，他们成为地方与全球相互连通的节点。

与此同时，农业现代化导致农村就业机会减少，这也是促使人们迁往城市的另一个因素。

地缘政治和冲突影响着城市化和城市发展。第二次世界大战以来，随着联合国和其他政府间机构的成立，一种复杂的多层次磋商、管理和治理体系已经形成，这也对城市治理和管理产生了影响。尽管建立了维持和平的国际机构，但冲突仍是跨国移居的一个原因。此外，人们还会因气候变化而离开无法找到合适生活条件的地区或国家。

从国际层面来看，新兴国家（新兴市场七国：中国、印度、巴西、墨西哥、俄罗斯、印度尼西亚和土耳其）在全球舞台获得了更多的政治权力和影响力，由此形成了一个多极化的全球政治体系。从地方层面来看，许多国家的城市拥有了越来越多的自主权，城市治理和管理正在发挥重要作用，市长成为变革的主要推动者。

"人口结构变化的诱发因素包括移民（农村人口流入城市和跨国移居）以及预期寿命和出生率的逐渐变化。"[1] 全球人口正在增加，到 2050 年预计将攀升至 93 亿，这种增长主要集中在发展中国家。

生活条件得到改善，将会导致死亡率下降和人口老龄化。这些发展将会对劳动力市场、住房、服务、消费模式以及提供充足的养老服务产生重要影响。

由于"城市是社会、文化、经济、技术和政治变革与进步的推动者"，城市化能够带来诸多积极影响和机遇[2]，比如发展经济、增加就业机会、建设新市场、提高生产力、享受邻近之便利、降低运输成本，城市将会成为提供综合服务、教育和医疗保健、创新、文化和创造力的中心，并可加强地方与全球的连通性。

城市化和城市发展的机遇和挑战需通过按照国际层面定义

---

[1] O. Courtard, G. Finnveden, S. Kabitsch, R. Kitchin, R. Matos, P. Nijkamp, C. Pronello, D. Robinson, Urban Megatrends: Towards a European Research Agenda: A Report by the Scientific Advisory Board of the Joint Programming Initiative Urban Europe, 2014, p. 5.

[2] Q. Z. Zhang:《世界城市化的趋势、承诺和挑战》,《国际城乡居住杂志》2016 年第 54 期。

和约定的可持续发展要求，针对具体情况而设计的政策、计划和行动纲领加以解决。

虽然一般而言各大洲的城市面临着同样挑战，但实现城市可持续发展需要考虑城市的具体情况，预测其文化、基础设施、经济、社会特征和动态。此外，规模也很重要，大城市和中小城镇之间同样存在巨大差异。另外，城市所面临的挑战正在将其转变为迈向可持续发展的前沿阵地，以及"展开有效环保行动的特权地带"①。

总的来说，城市领导及政府应充分遵循符合全球协议和目标的国家战略框架，制定新战略并采用新的管理方法来解决复杂问题、创造新机遇。

城市化带来了巨大的环境挑战，其中的驱动因素包括工业活动、交通、建设活动、供暖、能源需求增加、各种废弃物处理、卫生、空气污染、水土、土地利用、城市扩张、缺乏绿地或绿地退化等。

城市可持续发展还可能出现各种挑战和问题，需尽可能地通过城市发展的系统规划和管理加以解决，比如②：（1）城市

---

① UN-Habitat, *Urbanization and Development*：*Emerging Future. Key Findings and Messages*, *World Cities Report 2016*, United Nations Human Settlements Programme (UN-Habitat), 2016, p. 18.

② 参见 Q. Z. Zhang《世界城市化的趋势、承诺和挑战》，《国际城乡居住杂志》2016 年第 54 期。

扩张、土地管理问题、土地利用、城市农业、土地和生态系统退化；（2）中心与边缘差异、通勤时间、服务分配不均；（3）缺乏足够的住房投资，导致经济适用房短缺，出现贫民窟；（4）生活成本增高、失业风险、贫困风险和社会排斥；（5）城市不平等和性别不平等、贫富差距、社会隔离、女孩和妇女与男孩和妇女相比受到的不平等影响更深；（6）基础设施投资短缺、安全供水不足、废物管理和处理问题（私人和工业）、污水处理、缺乏足够的卫生服务；（7）交通拥堵以及汽车、工业和火力供暖的废气排放；（8）环境恶化，特别是水、空气和土壤污染、噪音和光线胁迫，温室气体排放，废物管理和处理问题；（9）犯罪和不安全、地区变得无法控制、封闭社区增多和私人安保服务造成隔离，并导致不同社会群体之间的不信任增加。

需要强调的是，这些挑战均相互依存，需采取系统化方法加以解决。

城市可能缺乏足够的资源来完成必要任务，应对众多挑战。发展中国家的城市化已成为一种持续存在的重要现象；根据预测，未来90%以上的城市增长都将出现在发展中国家①。

---

① Q. Z. Zhang：《世界城市化的趋势、承诺和挑战》，《国际城乡居住杂志》2016年第54期。

然而，地区和国家之间也将出现极大差异。在发达国家，大城市的人口将会减少，而中小城市的人口将会增多，从而出现一种平衡过程。发展中国家的特点是大城市正在吸引更多的人口，"最大限度地发挥积极的外部效应、尽量减少负面影响"①成为各国政府和市政当局的一项挑战。

三　全球城市可持续发展框架和最新成果

就全球而言，城市化在应对全球社会挑战方面的变革力量已在最近的全球政策、议程和指导方针中得到认可和明确表述。联合国在《2030 年可持续发展议程》中制定了 17 项可持续发展目标，以"促使人们在今后 15 年内，在那些对人类和地球至关重要的领域中采取行动"②。城市地区对实现可持续发展目标的重要性显而易见，从它们在文件里的突出作用中可见一斑："可持续发展目标 11"完全针对的是可持续城市和社区，而所有 17 个可持续发展目标均有城市方面的内容。此外，

---

① UN-Habitat, *Urbanization and Development*: *Emerging Future*. Key Findings and Messages, *World Cities Report 2016*, United Nations Human Settlements Programme (UN-Habitat), 2016, p. 41.

② United Nations, Transforming our World: The 2030 Agenda for Sustainable Development, 2015, https://sustainabledevelopment. un. org/post2015/transformingourworld, p. 3.

169 项指标中有 90 项包括城市地区。17 项可持续发展目标及其指标明显强调了可持续城市化对于人类和地球未来的重要性。

"可持续发展目标 11"首次明确了从全球层面讨论可持续城市化与城市发展在政治、政策和实践中的必要性。联合国人居署根据"可持续发展目标 11"发布了《新城市议程》，几乎所有成员国都已签署。《新城市议程》阐明了城市化的共同愿景，以期打造可持续的未来，为所有人创造福利和机会。最重要的是，《新城市议程》标志着一种思考模式的转变：将城市可持续发展当作社会挑战的一种解决方案。"可持续发展目标 11"和《新城市议程》正在为具有全球共识的可持续路径目标和愿景提供一种全球参考框架①。

> （"可持续发展目标 11"和《新城市议程》）指出城市不只是问题和风险的温床，更是社会进步的驱动力，这可被视为一种思考模式的转变。城市发展对于实现可持续发展目标至关重要，这是因为全球一半以上的人口现都居住在城市地区，而且这一数字还在继续增长②。

---

① JPI Urban Europe Scientific Advisory Board, New Urban Transitions towards Sustainability, Manuscript in preparation, 2018.

② Ibid. .

　　"可持续发展目标 11"和《新城市议程》中的愿景和路径与思考模式的转变有关：将城市化视为一个具有变革力量的过程①，而不是引发环境和社会挑战及问题的不良变化。然而，实现可持续转型的方法具有多方面和多样化的特点，涉及各方面的活动、方法、计划、项目、利益攸关方和倡议。实现城市政策以及研究和创新方法的多样性②，需要探索不同的领域、方法和技术，分析它们的综合影响并挖掘其变革潜力③，继而推进城市转型。与此同时，还需弄清相互冲突的目标、战略和需求，以免它们阻塞变革力量，继而限制城市转型。

　　实现城市可持续发展存在多种途径，可根据特定城市地区的具体情况重点关注某些目标。在可持续发展目标发布的同一年，Hassan 和 Lee④调查了过去 5 年全球发表的科学论文

---

①　Foreword by Joan Clos：UN-Habitat, National Urban Policy：A Guiding Framework, 2015, https：//unhabitat. org/books/national-urban-policy-a-guiding-framework/.

②　城市转型的定义为"城市发展的根本性和多维度转变，通过避免对环境以及经济和自然资源的公平分配造成更大压力，实现保障公民生计的宏伟目标"；JPI UE：SRIA Strategic Research and Innovation Agenda, 2015, https：//jpi-urbaneurope. eu/documents_ library/.

③　Bylund, J. , Connecting the Dots by Obstacles？ Friction and Traction Ahead for the SRIA Urban Transitions Pathway, Joint Programming Initiative Urban Europe, 2016.

④　A. M. Hassan & H. Lee, "Toward the Sustainable Development of Urban Areas：An Overview of Global Trends in Trials and Policies", *Land us Policy*, 48, 2015.

中与城市可持续发展高度相关的文献研究课题，并归类如下：
（1）城市可持续发展和社会文化意识的平衡方法；（2）经济可持续性与减少温室气体；（3）城市结构、土地利用、城市扩张和可持续交通；（4）经济城市发展；（5）城市更新、城市绿地和可持续评估系统；（6）评估城市可持续性，推广城市发展经验。

研究特别指出，根据所调查的出版物，就数量和质量而言，交通和教育意识是首要关注点。研究人员一致认为，交通政策可为创造城市可持续性做出重要贡献，措施包括推广电动汽车或对特定区域征收通行费，以及投资扩建公共交通网络等。此外，家庭和工作之间的联系、居民优化居住空间（通勤和工作方面）的可能性等方面缺乏研究。

该研究总结认为，欧洲在促进城市可持续发展方面最先迈步，并在亚洲之前达到了可接受的城市可持续发展水平。就亚洲而言，城市可持续发展现已成为国家的重要议程，中国在关注城市可持续发展方面排名第一，印度第二。

在欧洲，数量和质量问题主要集中在重建历史建筑方面，比如提高它们的能源效率。科学出版物认为社会参与和教育意识非常重要。在亚洲，科学文献从数量方面指出的重要问题包括：土地利用、可持续性评估、城市扩张、交通、教育意识、城市绿地建设，以及制定一种综合经济、社会和生态问题的平衡方法的必要性。就质量而言，亚洲最突出的问题是教育意识、社会参与和城市土地利用。在美国、拉丁美洲和澳大利亚 3 个地区中，美国对城市可持续发展的认识最深。美国、加拿大和澳大利亚都在努力控制汽车数量，以减少温室气体排放。在美国，城市农业已被列入议程，作为实现城市自给自足目标的一项措施。由于大多数非洲国家的经济和政治条件恶劣，因此非洲有关城市可持续发展的研究活动极少。

值得注意的是，科学文献的分析结果中缺少许多重要方面，比如（仅举几例）建筑物、社会经济以及治理角色。

在可持续发展目标达成一致大约 3 年后，联合国有关"可持续发展目标 11"实施情况的报告如下①。

"可持续发展目标 11"：建设包容、安全、有抵御灾害能力和可持续的城市和人类住区

城市增长的步伐前所未有。2015 年，将近 40 亿人（占世界人口的一半以上）生活在城市；然而，虽然城市孵化了创新，促进了就业和经济增长，但快速的城市化也

---

① United Nations, *The Sustainable Development Goals Report 2017*, New York, 2017, p. 8.

带来了巨大挑战，其中包括住房不足、空气污染加剧以及缺乏基本服务和基础设施等。

全球生活在贫民窟的城市人口占比从 2000 年的 28% 下降到了 2014 年的 23%。但在撒哈拉以南非洲，超过一半（56%）的城市居民生活在贫民窟。

2000—2015 年，世界各地城市土地的扩张超过了城市人口的增长，由此导致了城市无序扩张。

根据 2009—2013 年 101 个国家的城市数据，大约 65% 的城市人口享受到了城市垃圾收集服务。

2014 年，9/10 的城市居民呼吸的空气不符合世界卫生组织颗粒物（PM 2.5）方面的空气质量标准。

截至 2017 年 5 月，149 个国家完全或部分实施了国家层面的城市政策，其中大多数与可持续发展目标所确定的优先领域一致。

四　报告的目的

该报告旨在通过分析城市可持续发展方面的主要挑战，介绍欧洲和中国部分城市的优秀案例，从而对进一步的需求和优先事项做出展望。

五 报告的结构

该报告共分五章。第一章将从城市化、可持续发展目标和《新城市议程》的背景简述城市可持续发展，为研究奠定基础。第二章将阐述与城市可持续发展相关的全球趋势、主要挑战和主要成就。第三章将分析欧洲和中国城市可持续发展的主要挑战和战略（方法）。第四章将论述欧洲和中国所选城市的优秀案例，重点关注五个专题。第五章将总结欧洲和中国城市可持续发展的现有合作项目，并对进一步的需求和优先事项做出展望。

第二章　欧洲和中国城市可持续发展的主要挑战和战略、方法

一　欧洲的主要挑战和战略、方法

1. 欧洲政策和计划内容

欧洲的城市化模式与世界其他地区存在极大差别。欧洲的城市化程度更高，约73%的人口居住在城市地区。欧洲的城市化具有一个鲜明特征，即与亚洲、南美和北美相比，其拥有大量的中小城市，而居住人口超过100万的城市地区相对较少。① 全球共有79个城市的人口超过500万，但欧洲只占4个。欧洲16%的居民生活在人口超过500万的城市之中，而

---

① JPI Urban Europe, Strategic Research and Innovation Agenda, 2015, https://jpi-urbaneurope.eu/documents_library/.

亚洲的这个数字为30%，北美为28%①。

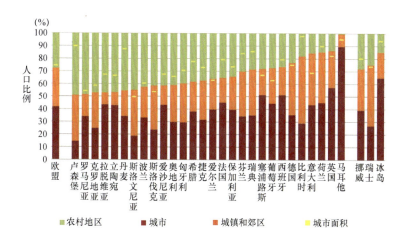

图3　2014年欧盟各国城市化程度人口数据

资料来源：European Commission and UN-Habitat：The State of the European Cities，2016；Eurostat and World Urbanization Propstects，2014。

　　欧洲城市地区的形式、组织、空间动态、社会经济结构和治理体系各不相同。这些差异具有历史原因，且是由国家和地方层面的组织轨迹和政治形态所决定的，东南欧和西北欧国家的城市发展也由此形成对比。然而，欧洲和全球的影响将

① European Commission and UN-HABITAT，The State of the European Cities，2016，http：//ec. europa. eu/regional ＿ policy/en/policy/themes/urban-development/cities-report/。

"最终需要融入复杂的地方条件和要求，以便根据实际情况采取应对措施（表现改进战略）"①。

优先领域的确定考虑了欧洲城市的表现②以及《2030 年可持续发展目标》新的政策框架，它们也是进一步推动欧洲城市地区发展的关键。这些主题已被纳入《欧盟城市议程》的相关工作。《欧盟城市议程》（"阿姆斯特丹条约"）旨在解决欧盟以及各国政策和立法中的城市相关问题，是一种具有协调性和综合性的方法。因此，公共机关、成员国、欧洲委员会以及非政府组织或企业等利益攸关方共同组建了 12 个主题伙伴关系。这些伙伴关系的主题包括智能土地使用、气候适应、循环经济、移民和难民包容、城市出行、住房、空气质量、城市贫困、地方经济中的就业和技能、数字转型和公共采购等。《欧盟城市议程》旨在落实和实施联合国人居署的《新城市议程》，由欧盟委员会负责。

欧洲已做出巨大努力的领域（重要方法、主题领域和挑战）包括智慧城市和社区、气候变化、难民和移民融合等。智慧城市和社区是指越来越多地利用信息通信技术，并使（社会）创新发挥重要作用的城市地区。这一概念中，信息通

---

① JPI Urban Europe, Strategic Research and Innovation Agenda, 2015.

② As described extensively in: European Commission and UN-HABITAT, The State of the European Cities, 2016.

信技术可成为应对社会挑战、促进社会参与城市发展的主要推动因素。特别重视包括社会过程的技术方法——简而言之就是创新与社会之间的联系——促使智慧城市和社区成为城市化的重要概念。此外，欧洲城市已做出极大努力来减排温室气体，其中包括提高现有建筑的能源效率。减缓气候变化的战略和方法拥有一个共同特征。适应气候变化方面，自然湿地、绿地网络以及社区和建筑绿化等自然化解决方案最近已引起广泛关注①。2015 年夏以来，许多欧洲国家——尤其是城市地区——都成了大量难民的目的地，融合和积极包容他们已变得越来越重要。这种融合需要各方努力，包括教育系统、住房部门和劳动力市场展开创新。

除了欧洲委员会及其成员国资助和支持的举措之外，欧洲在可持续城市化方面还存在许多相关的参与者和网络：国际地方政府环境行动理事会②（地方政府可持续发展协会）、欧洲城市组织③（欧洲主要城市的所选地方和城市政府网络）、欧洲区域研究与创新网络④、欧洲市政和地区理事会⑤以及联合

---

① European Commission and UN-HABITAT, The State of the European Cities, 2016.

② http://iclei-europe.org/home/.

③ http://www.eurocitics.cu/.

④ https://www.errin.eu/.

⑤ http://www.ccre.org/.

国人居署（欧洲）①。

2. 欧洲城市计划——为城市转型提供支持的研究和创新计划

近年来，城市发展在欧洲受到越来越多的关注。城市地区是各个地区——甚至是国家和欧洲大陆——发展和创新的枢纽。城市既是难民和移民的避难所，也是适应气候变化和可持续发展的区域，因此在解决许多社会挑战问题中扮演着关键角色。正如导言部分所指出的，城市地区在实现联合国《2030 年可持续发展议程》的 17 个可持续发展目标方面均发挥着至关重要的作用，而不仅仅是在目标 11 "可持续城市和社区" 方面。

欧洲城市计划致力于通过资助战略研究和创新、改进和调整研究及创新工具、调整科学政策过程、为跨国合作提供支持和促进地方能力建设，解决城市转型的复杂问题。欧洲城市计划可将政府当局、民间团体、科学家、创新者、工商业界联系在一起，为城市研究和创新提供一个良好的环境，其使命是为城市转型对话开发工具、知识和平台。

作为对未来可持续和宜居城市转型这个核心主题的一种补充，2015 年出版的欧洲城市计划《战略研究和创新议程》还提出了五个需要解决的优先主题，即增强城市经济活力、福利

---

① https：//unhabitat. org/tag/europe/.

和金融、环境可持续性和韧性、可达性和连接性、城市治理和参与。

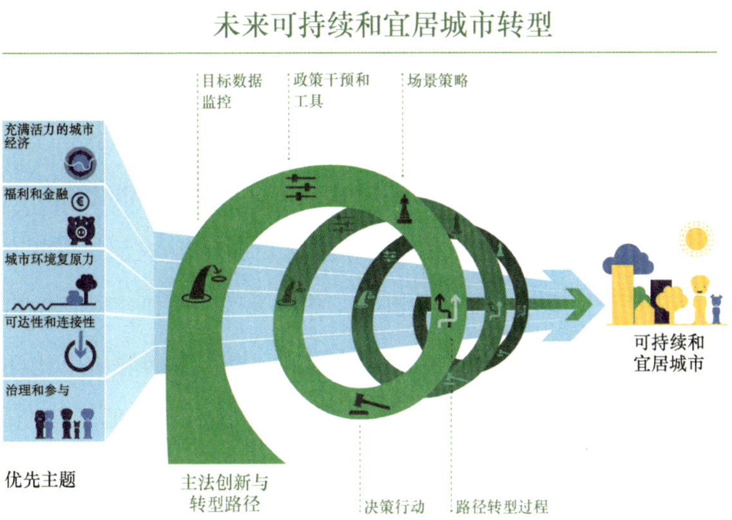

未来可持续和宜居城市转型

图4 欧洲城市计划《战略研究和创新议程》框架

实施过程中，20个欧洲国家的政府和资助组织成员正在根据每个国家的城市发展计划和活动，联手开展了若干联合行动。从这个意义上说，欧洲城市计划已成为一个贯通和完善这些计划、吸收跨国经验和能力的平台。目标是提供一个创新生态系统，促使公共和社会行动者参与使命履行和解决方案的提出，创建新型伙伴关系，应对城市挑战。

二　中国的主要挑战和战略、方法

1978 年改革开放以来的 40 年间，中国亲历了前所未有的快速城市化发展。其城市化率已从 1979 年[①]的 18.96% 增至 2010 年的 51.27%，2017 年达到 58.52%，城市总人口达 8.1347 亿[②]。在此过程中，中国成功避开了快速城市化常见的一些负面影响（比如城市贫困和失业），2.6 亿农民工[③]在城市地区第二、第三产业中找到了工作，为经济的快速增长做出了贡献，5 亿中国人口也由此摆脱了贫困[④]。中国的城市化尚未完成——根据目前的人均收入，城市人口占比仍低于预期。按照目前的趋势，中国 2030 年的城市化率预计将达 65%，每年均有 2000 万人口进入城市地区居住[⑤]。

中国农村人口流入城市的规模空前，背后的主要推动力是

[①]　联合国人居署：《2010/2011 中国城市状况报告：城市，让生活更美好》，外文出版社 2010 年版。

[②]　中国国家统计局。

[③]　"农民工"是指在农村地区注册或持有农村户口，但进入城市地区生活和工作的人们。一般而言，农民工无法像在城市地区注册或持有城市户口的居民一样获得城市公共服务。

[④]　世界银行和国务院发展研究中心：《中国：推进高效、包容、可持续的城镇化》，2014 年。

[⑤]　同上。

工业化快速发展，其城市发展模式的特点是城区加速扩展、能源消耗量大[①]。城市化加速发展的过程中，城市人口快速增长导致城市迅速扩张，这已成为经济增长的重要推动力，并为利益攸关方带来了巨大利益[②]。但与此同时，快速的城区扩展和人口增长也为城市可持续发展带来了各种挑战，比如城市扩张、交通拥堵、能源消耗过度和环境恶化等[③]。

这些挑战非常复杂且相互交织，主要是因为中国经济的快速增长是由投资来推动，而且过去几十年来城市化过度依赖于土地流转和土地融资[④]。这在某种程度上反映在过去 30 年来典型的城市发展模式中，即大规模城市街区的单一用途区域[⑤]。城市中心许多传统的住宅社区已被拆除，居民搬迁到了正在进行新城镇建设（目的是将工作机会和住房供给迁出城

---

① 魏后凯：《新时期中国城镇化转型战略》，《城市转型与绿色发展（中国经济论坛 2012 文集）》，中国社会科学出版社 2014 年版。

② Tan, Y.、Xu, H.、Zhang, X.：《中国可持续城镇化：城市文献综述》2016 年第 55 期。

③ 仇保兴（2016 年）：《新型城镇化的新视角》，http://kns.cnki.net/KCMS/detail/detail.aspx? dbcode = CFJD&dbname = CJFDTFMN&filename = ZFGP201600007&v = MjY1NTBoMVQzcVRyV00xRnJDVVJMJMS2ZaT1JyRnlIblVMelBQeXZNZnJHNE g5Zk1yNDlGWTRSOGVYMUx1eFlTN0Q = 。

④ 联合国人居署：《2010/2011 中国城市状况报告：城市，让生活更美好》，外文出版社 2010 年版。

⑤ Wang, J. and He, D., "Sustainable Urban Development in China: Challenges and Achievements", *Mitigation and Adaptation Strategies for Global Change*, 20, 2015, pp. 665 – 682.

市中心）的郊区。但实际上，城市中心的人口密度并未减少。与此相反，这些多用途开发还不完善的郊区逐渐与城市中心连为一体，造成了城市扩张。这些地方道路宽阔，但多式联运和地方道路发展不足、公共交通连接不畅，使得问题更加严重。由此导致的结果是城市中心与郊区之间的主干道和高速公路交通流量增加，加剧了对汽车的依赖、交通拥堵、消耗能源以及其他方面的城市挑战。

中国的政策制定者和决策者越来越认识到这些挑战及其负面影响，并对此给予了极大关注。中国已采取各种战略、方法来应对这些挑战，这体现于一些重大事件，以及为应对中国快速城市化带来的挑战而制定的环境保护和可持续发展政策。比如，国务院1983年召开第二次全国环境保护会议，将环境保护确立为基本国策。1992年，国务院发布了《中国环境与发展十大对策》，针对中国的可持续发展提出了具体措施。1997年，中共十五大将可持续发展确立为国家的现代化建设战略。2007年，党的十七大首次提出"生态文明"的概念，其中涉及环境保护和可持续发展。2015年，《中国环境保护法》修订版开始施行，要求企业承担更多的污染防治责任，加大了环境污染处罚力度，建立了环境公益诉讼制度。表1归纳了中国自20世纪70年代以来，与环境保护和可持续发展相关的重大事件和政策。

表1　　中国环境保护与可持续发展方面的重大事件和

政策（20世纪70年代至今）

年份	政策	事件/发布机构	要点/意义
1973	《关于保护和改善环境的若干规定》	国务院委托国家计委召开第一次全国环境保护会议	确定了与规划、资源利用和公众参与环境保护相关的原则，标志着当代中国环境保护工作的开始
1979	《中国环境保护法（试行）》	全国人大常委会	是中国遵照《中华人民共和国宪法》（1978年修订）制定的第一部环境保护法
1982	《中华人民共和国宪法》（1982年修订）	全国人民代表大会	是中华人民共和国的根本大法；第一次将环境保护、污染防治和自然资源保护纳入其中
1982	国民经济和社会发展"六五"计划	国务院	独章论述环境保护，将环境保护确定为政府面临的十大主要任务之一
1983		国务院召开第二次全国环境保护会议	将环境保护列为国家战略，极大提高了公众的环保意识，制定了适合中国的环境保护总体指导方针
1989	《1989—1992年环境保护目标和任务》《全国2000年环境保护规划纲要》	国务院召开第三次全国环境保护会议	评价了当前的环境保护形势，总结了三大环境政策的成功经验；提出了新的五项制度和措施，形成了中国环境管理的"八项制度"
1989	《中国环境保护法》（1989年修订）	全国人大常委会	修订后的法律包含了上述制度，夯实了环境保护的法律基础

年份	政策	事件/发布机构	要点/意义
1992	《中国环境与发展十大对策》	国务院	是针对中国可持续发展制定的具体措施; 是中国环境保护与发展方面的指导性文件
1994	《中国 21 世纪议程:中国 21 世纪人口、环境与发展白皮书》	国务院	中国 21 世纪议程提出,应将本政策所提及的目标和内容纳入国民经济和社会发展计划和长期计划; 将可持续发展的概念和目标纳入中国国家层面的决策过程,这是一个重要起点
1996	《关于保护和改善环境的若干规定》	国务院召开第四次全国环境保护会议	将环境保护确定为可持续发展战略中最重要的任务,开启了中国环境保护的新篇章
1996	《国家环境保护"九五"计划和 2010 年远景目标》	国家环保总局	是"九五"（1996—2000 年）期间以及 2010 年之前 15 年的环境保护指导性文件
1997		党的十五大	可持续发展被确立为国家现代化战略
2001	《国家环境保护"十五"计划》	国家环保总局	包含了《主要污染物总量控制规划》和《中国绿色工程规划（第二期）》; 是第十个五年计划（2001—2005 年）期间的环境保护指导性文件
2002		国务院召开第五次全国环境保护会议	为"十五"期间国家环境保护计划的实施做出安排; 提出环境保护是政府的一项重要职能,应动员全社会的力量做好这项工作

续表

年份	政策	事件/发布机构	要点/意义
2003	《中华人民共和国环境影响评价法》	全国人大常委会	旨在预防各种规划和建设项目的实施对环境造成不良影响，实现可持续发展； 是实施可持续发展战略的重要法律基础
2005	《国家环境保护"十一五"规划》	国家环保总局和国家发改委	是第十一个五年计划（2006—2010 年）期间的环境保护指导性文件
2006	《环境行政处罚办法（试行）》	国家环保总局	旨在惩处违法行为，促进环境保护法律法规的实施； 是加强环境保护和管理的一项重大政策
2006		国务院召开第六次全国环境保护会议	对环境保护和管理的态度提出"三个转变"：①保护环境与经济增长并重，②环境保护与经济发展同步，③综合运用法律、经济、技术和必要的行政办法解决环境问题； "三个转变"对于在环境保护的新时代实现环境目标具有重要意义
2007	"十七大"报告	党的十七大	正式提出了"生态文明"的概念； 涉及环境保护和可持续发展
2007	《环境信息公开办法（试行）》	国家环保总局	旨在规范如何向公众披露环境信息； 指出鼓励公众参与环境保护是一项重要政策
2011	《国务院关于加强环境保护重点工作的意见》	国务院召开第七次全国环境保护会议	强调通过加强环境保护管理、加强环境执法监督等方式提高实施效率

年份	政策	事件/发布机构	要点/意义
2011	《国家环境保护"十二五"规划》	生态环境部	是第十二个五年计划（2011—2015年）期间的环境保护指导性文件
2014	《中国环境保护法》（2014年修订）	全国人大常委会	是最新的环境保护法，于2015年1月1日开始实施
2016	《国家环境保护"十三五"规划》	生态环境部	是第十三个五年计划（2016—2020年）期间的环境保护指导性文件

资料来源：笔者整理。

2002 年，联合国人居署/国际发展部根据可持续发展的原则，提出将可持续城市化作为一个重要组成部分，其特点是实现可持续发展原则的城市化进程①。可持续城市化是实现中国城市可持续发展的一种有效途径，有助于应对快速城市化进程带来的诸多挑战②。世界银行和国务院发展研究中心 2014 年进行的一项联合研究表明，中国需从传统模式转变为更高效、

---

① 联合国人居署/国际发展部：《可持续城市化：实现"21 世纪议程"》，内罗比：联合国人居署/国际发展部，2002 年。

② Tan, Y.、Xu, H.、Zhang, X.：《中国可持续城镇化：城市文献综述》2016 年第 55 期；Zhao, P.，Sustainable Urban Expansion and Transportation in a Growing Megacity: Consequences of Urban Sprawl for Mobility on the Urban Fringe of Beijing, *Habitat International*, 34（2），2010，pp. 236 – 243。

更具包容性和可持续性的城市化新模式。此处，"'有效城市化'能最有效地利用中国的生产资料——人民、土地和资本；'包容性城市化'能为所有人提供受益于城市化的平等机会——将劳动力用于最有生产力的地方，不断积累资产和储蓄，提供同等质量的公共服务；'可持续城市化'意味着中国的环境（土地、空气、水）和自然资源可为城市化提供支持，同时提供符合中国人民愿望的城市生活质量"[1]。

2013 年，中共十八届三中全会通过了《中共中央关于全面深化改革若干重大问题的决定》（以下简称《决定》），提出了中国特色新型城镇化的概念（以下简称"新型城镇化"）[2]。《决定》提出要完善城镇化健康发展体制机制，推进以人为核心的城镇化；推动大中小城市和小城镇协调发展、产业和城镇融合发展；促进城镇化和新农村建设协调推进。《决定》还提出要优化城市空间结构和管理格局，增强城市综合承载能力。新型城镇化充分考虑了中国国情以及在快速城市化过程中从传统转向更科学发展方式的必要性[3]，体现了可持续城市化和城市化新模式的概念。

---

[1]　世界银行和国务院发展研究中心：《中国：推进高效、包容、可持续的城镇化》，2014 年。

[2]　http://www.china.org.cn/chinese/2014-01/17/content_31226494.htm.

[3]　仇保兴：《新型城镇化的新视角》，2016 年。

　　许多试点项目已在"新型城镇化"领域开始实施，如更紧凑和多用途开发，更有效的能源使用和废物管理等。一些试点项目已成为优秀案例，正在推广实施，这有助于解决全国城市面临的挑战。下一章将按六个专题来介绍中国的优秀案例，即可持续城市规划和城市更新、能效与低碳发展、交通出行、城市更新与城市固体废物管理、共享经济与私营部门贡献、智慧城市治理。

第三章 中欧优秀案例

一 可持续城市规划和城市更新

1. 概述

以人为本进行城市规划、增加现有住宅的能源效率、提高居民的生活质量是城市可持续发展的关键。为此，SubUrban-Lab 项目展示了城市创新应用实验室如何通过协同设计与参与式规划，对贫困社区进行现代化改造，从而提升其社会地位。中国城市超级街区的发展影响了城市地区的可步行性，促进了城市扩张。四川南充的大规模更新项目说明城市规划和更新有助于促进人类规模发展，构建多中心城市结构，提高可步行性和公园可及性，为建设可持续的宜居城市地区做出贡献。

2. 欧洲案例研究

欧洲城市计划项目：SubUrbanLab

SubUrbanLab 旨在研究市政当局如何联合当地居民和其他

利益攸关方，共同实现贫困社区和郊区的现代化和社会振兴，将这些郊区建设成为更具吸引力、更可持续和更具经济可行性的城市地区。该项目在瑞典和芬兰的两个郊区建立了城市创新应用实验室，探索动员居民和利益攸关方积极参与城市环境改造的新手段。

（1）利益攸关方参与地方升级

全欧洲约有 2 亿人居住在郊区，这些地方拥有大型住宅区，且急需实现现代化和社会振兴。这些地区的价值较低，那里通常拥有大型建筑，当地环境缺乏吸引力，而且居民大都属于社会和经济弱势群体。在瑞典和芬兰，这些地区一直是政府计划和改革方案的实施对象，以期改善公共空间、提高建筑能效、改善废物管理，并通过动员当地居民参与地方建设增强社会凝聚力和对地方政府的信任。试点和测试解决方案正在成为所选方法的共同特点。

（2）城市创新应用实验室

2014—2016 年，芬兰国家技术研究中心（VTT）、瑞典环境科学研究院（IVL）与瑞典的布特许尔卡市（Botkyrka）、芬兰的里希迈基市（Riihimäki）共同合作，开展了 SubUrbanLab 项目。该项目共在瑞典和芬兰开发和建设了 6 个城市创新应用实验室。

城市创新应用实验室能够利用各种协同设计方案来了解利

益攸关方的需求，提出和展示想法，并在实践中评估解决方案。它是一个可为城市地区开发新产品、新系统、新服务和新流程的创新平台。城市创新应用实验室将人作为整个开发过程的核心，他们既是用户，也是共创者。人们在此可以测试、探索、诊查、试验和评估新的想法，从而在复杂的日常环境中提出创造性解决方案。2012 年以来，欧洲城市计划资助的 67 个项目中近一半都具有城市创新应用实验室的元素，现已有大量项目组合正在不同的环境和背景下测试城市创新应用实验室。

这个项目研究了如何利用城市创新应用实验室，促使两个郊区（瑞典的奥尔比和芬兰的里希迈基）的居民及其他利益攸关方参与郊区和地方社区的现代化和社会振兴，共同开发和测试日常生活中的新服务或解决方案。新服务或解决方案的用户是整个开发过程中的积极参与者，这些开发均发生在真实的城市环境里。从以下两个城市创新应用实验室的描述中，可看出这项研究是如何关注规模相对较小的项目，为合作提供机会的。

"New light on Alby Hill" 主要研究的是如何改造人行道，使其更具吸引力和更安全。研究人员、公共组织、公司、非政府组织和居民一起进行规划、设计和安装了人行道环境照明和灯光设施，并以"我们的奥尔比"为主题设计了灯光装置图案。获奖图案最终通过公开投票产生。社会和环境可持续性建

Vote for your favorite image!

During the autumn we asked for images to be used for lightening up stonewalls along a walkway on Albyberget. 20 images were submitted and we have chosen six to be part of the final voting. The two winning images will light up one stonewall each. **Vote for YOUR favorite image now!**

You can vote by using the QR-code or via the website **www.nyttljus.eu**

You can vote until the 8th of March.

1. *Peace –*
Brandy Contreras
Sanchez and
Oulaymatou Jallow

2. *Alby i mitt hjärta –*
Jannika Ojeda Meftah

3. *Nej till rasism – Jasmine Icke*

4. *Höghus – Lema Murad*

5. *Vi är lika – Tamona*

6. *Vårt Alby – Mirac Yavuz och Rami Khalil*

Ett samarbete
"Nytt ljus på Albyberget" är ett samarbete mellan Botkyrka kommun, Mitt Alby AB, Konstfack och IVL Svenska Miljöinstitutet. "Nytt ljus på Albyberget" är en del av projektet SubUrbanLab (suburbanlab.eu), och arbetet utför med bidrag från Vinnova inom ramen för JPI Urban Europe, och är det andra av tre Urban Living Lab (ULL) som kommer att genomföras i Alby.

图 5 城市创新应用实验室 "New light on Alby Hill" 海报

设不仅增加了安全感，为居民的持续参与奠定了基础，而且也实现了降低街道照明能耗等目标。

佩尔托萨里（Peltosaari）的"Together more"为居民提供了参与环境规划建设和安排地方活动的机会，目标在于改善该地区的外貌景致，增强居民的集体认同感。这个项目试点开展了几种活动，动员居民参与讨论地方计划。它还推出了设法吸引当地年轻人参加的新活动，加强了各群体间的合作。这个地区赢得了大量正面的新闻报道。

（3）6个城市创新应用实验室的关键成功因素以及主要经验和教训

城市创新应用实验室的关键成功因素包括受影响民众的早期和持续参与，拥有明确的目标和期望，以及将讨论付诸行动。这些方法必须符合目标和参与者的需求。最好的情况是人们愿意参与城市创新应用实验室的各种活动以及其他活动，并在不久后亲眼见证自己的参与结果。

6个城市创新应用实验室收获了很多经验，其中一则经验是每个城市创新应用实验室都会随所设背景不断发生变化，意外事件和不同利益攸关方的影响也会对其产生影响。这个过程并非线形的，它们会因研究人员、决策者和公共组织、居民和公司参与各个城市创新应用实验室的共建，而发生意想不到的变化。

项目所得教训包括如何更好地鼓励当地居民和市政当局参

与。这个项目还展示了用户驱动型城市创新应用实验室（主要由居民运行）该如何进一步加深居民对参与地方社会的感受；而对于推动者驱动型城市创新应用实验室（主要由市政运行）来说，如果完全采取创新应用实验室的工作方法并将其融入现有的组织惯例，那么就有可能获得足够的资源。

（4）边界条件和对城市的指导意义

通过查阅文献和居民访谈了解过去的利益攸关方参与经验，确定了建立城市创新应用实验室时需要考虑的要素和边界条件。城市创新应用实验室的边界条件以问题清单的形式呈现，其中包括针对五个要素（见图6）分别提出的问题（需在开展城市创新应用实验室活动之前回答），以及实际的答题示例和答题建议。

"SuburbanLab 项目获得的最大成果是我们能确定（普遍适用的）城市创新应用实验室的边界条件和关键成功因素，从而为其他城市提供明确指导，帮助它们建立类似的创新应用实验室。这些方法可被其他城市复制，但必须根据城市的具体需求来确定城市创新应用实验室的主题"，研究团队主管、芬兰国家技术研究中心（VTT）的科学博士（技术）Riikka Holopainen 表示。Riikka Holopainen 接着说道："参与奥尔比和里希迈基项目的地方利益攸关方也获益匪浅，当地环境和日常生活已变得更可持续"。

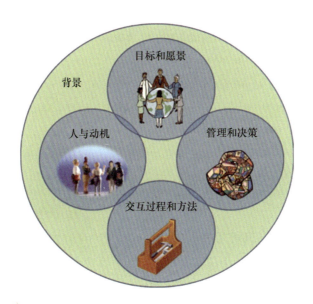

图 6　城市创新应用实验室规划五要素

资料来源：Bäck 等，2012 年。

（5）手册和指南①

手册《城市创新应用实验室：共创城市地区的竞技场》介绍的是成功因素和经验教训；报告《成功运行城市创新应用实验室的边界条件》② 针对的是希望创建城市创新应用实验室，以实现现代化和社会振兴的组织。

①　http：//suburbanlab. eu/wp-content/uploads/2016/05/SubUrbanLab_ booklet_ screen. pdf .

②　http：//suburbanlab. eu/tulokset/? lang = en.

SubUrbanLab——通过城市创新应用实验室，实现郊区的社会振奋和现代化

持续时间：2013—2016 年

网址：www. jpi-urbaneurope. eu/suburbanlab

联系方式：Riikka Holopainen，芬兰国家技术研究中心（VTT）有限公司

电子邮箱：riikka. holopainen@ vtt. fi

合作伙伴：瑞典环境科学研究院（IVL）、布特许尔卡市、里希迈基市、芬兰国家技术研究中心（VTT）有限公司

---

3. 中国案例研究

前面所提到的中国城市超级街区是导致步行非友好型建筑环境和交通拥堵的主要原因。进行更紧凑、多用途的开发有助于减轻城市扩张和对汽车的依赖，并提高基础设施、服务分配和交付中的可步行性及效率。

一些试点项目正在努力打造布局更小的街道网络，比如曹妃甸生态城和天津中新生态城（见图7）。后者的主要特点包括"公交导向型发展、混合土地利用、生态恢复、大型生态土地利用和湿地零净损失、可再生能源、智能电网、非传统水处理和再利用、垃圾清洁和利用、绿色交通和燃料、绿色建筑和生态工业园"[①]。

---

① Wang, J. and He, D., "Sustainable Urban Development in China: Challenges and Achievements", *Mitigation and Adaptation Strategies for Global Change*, 20, 2015, pp. 665 – 682.

图7 天津中新生态城的街道网络

资料来源：谷歌地球。

但与欧洲生态城相比——比如西班牙的巴塞罗那生态城，中国生态城的街道网格仍然较大。图8比较了中国曹妃甸生态城与西班牙巴塞罗那生态城拟建的人口尺度街道网络。

缩小街道网格的一种方法是重新开发可用于综合用途的棕色地带，增加可达性和绿色空间，将微观尺度融入现有的宏观尺度开发。图9的概念图显示了如何利用上述方法来细化粗糙网格。左图中的粉红多边形代表功能单一和以汽车为主导的街道网格，缺少步行友好性。通过添加公共交通网络和绿色廊道，现有粗糙网格细化之后的效果如右图所示。它们还可通过增设自行车和步行网络进一步细化。

因此，从土地利用的角度来看，可将粗糙网格的大块土地细化到人类尺度（见图 10），这样做可增加多样性和提高韧性，有利于城市的可持续发展。这些细化网格可被融入现有的城市地区，从而解决超级街区和城市扩张所带来的城市挑战。以下是中国南充的一个案例研究。

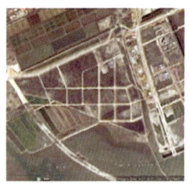

图 8　中国曹妃甸生态城（左）与西班牙巴塞罗那生态城（右）
拟建的人口尺度街道网络比较

资料来源：Wang, J. and He, D.，"Sustainable Urban Development in China: Challenges and Achievements"，*Mitigation and Adaptation Strategies for Global Change*，20，2015，pp. 665 –682。

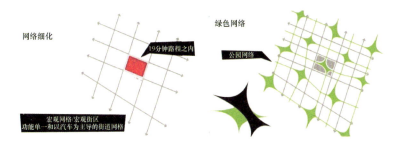

图9 方法概念图：将微观尺度融入现有的宏观尺度开发

资料来源：http://www.inktalks.com/discover/691/neville-mars-urban-renewal-of-mumbai-and-china。

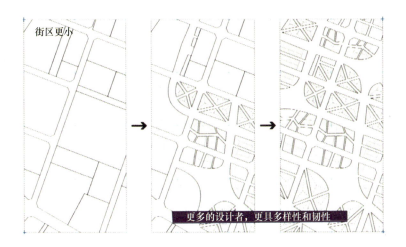

图10 方法应用的潜在影响：更具多样性和韧性

资料来源：http://www.inktalks.com/discover/691/neville-mars-urban-renewal-of-mumbai-and-china。

4. 案例研究——四川南充

南充是中国四川东北部一个地级市,位于嘉陵江中游,管辖3个区、5个县(营山县、西充县、南部县、蓬安县、仪陇县)和1个县级市,面积为12500平方千米,人口为760万[①]。2017年,顺庆、高坪和嘉陵3个城区的面积为126平方千米,人口为125万[②]。

2009年,南充启动了一项大型城市更新项目,涉及面积165万平方米,拆迁户3000户。这个项目翻新了历史建筑,为居民留下了寄托乡愁的遗产[③]。近年来,随着经济和交通的发展,该市的建筑环境和生态环境发生了巨大变化(见图11和图12)。

高坪区和嘉陵区商业中心的建设,再加上人口密度较高、道路网络和工业的发展,为南充打造出了多中心的城市结构。这有益于社会经济的可持续发展:2006—2015年的10年间,地区生产总值、城镇居民可支配收入和城市人口均在稳步增长。

---

① 顺庆区、高坪区、嘉陵;营山县、西充县、南部县、蓬安县、仪陇县;阆中市(县级市);参见 http://www.nanchong.gov.cn/10000/10004/10007/10030/2016/03/08/10127357.shtml。

② 参见 http://www.nanchong.gov.cn/10000/10004/10007/10030/2016/03/08/10127357.shtml。

③ 参见 http://nc.newssc.org/system/20161116/002057336_2.html。

图 11 《南充市核心城区交通改善规划》中的
道路系统、公交车道和步行网络

资料来源：http：//www. nanchong. gov. cn/10000/10003/10211/2015/03/06/
10118318. shtml。

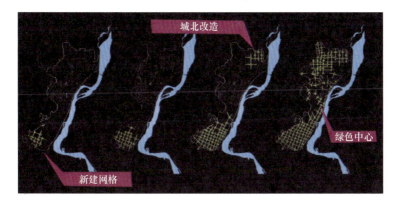

图 12 微观尺度逐步融入南充顺庆区和嘉陵区现有的宏观尺度开发

资料来源：http：//www. inktalks. com/discover/691/neville-mars-urban-renewal-
of-mumbai-and-china。

随着多中心结构的形成，南充的城市娱乐中心已扩展到了更多公园（如西河体育公园、南门坝生态公园和白塔公园）和步行网络。这已逐步将微观尺度融入了现有的宏观尺度开发，增加了可步行性和公园，南充居民受益匪浅，促进了城市的可持续发展。

二 能源效率和低碳发展

1. 概述

城市地区在减少温室气体排放和提高能源效率方面拥有巨大潜力，因此有助于采取减缓气候变化的行动。这不仅需要可再生能源技术或创新性能源管理，而且还需要改变用户行为。就此而言，项目 me² 旨在创建一个社区平台，以提高公民对能源消耗的认识，研究通过改变用户行为来提高能源效率的方法。阿姆斯特丹（荷兰）和里斯本（葡萄牙）的两个城市创新应用实验室对 me² 这个概念进行了测试。中国已从政策层面做出了努力。中国的几个部门通过制定生态城市政策、标准和低碳发展试点计划，促进了城市可持续发展。作为中国最好的案例之一，杭州实施了雄心勃勃的低碳城市计划，成为全国可持续发展的榜样。

2. 欧洲案例研究

欧洲城市计划项目：me^2

这个项目的亮点包括阿姆斯特丹和里斯本的试点项目、政策分析和调查结果以及 me^2 平台。它利用智能电网、电动交通、商业模式和政策激励，打造出了一个创新服务理念。

me^2 的目标是让公民更加了解能源消耗，激励个人和集体改变行为以节省电费，同时与当地社区建立联系。这个概念已在阿姆斯特丹和里斯本的两个城区试点项目中得到验证和优化。me^2 影响到了消费者、公用事业公司、电网运营商、电力供应商、市政当局和汽车共享公司。

"me^2 的整个实施过程在不断完善，我们一直在进行调整和微调"，阿姆斯特丹应用科学大学城市技术研究项目的项目经理、研究员 Halldora Thorsdottir 说道。

对一个社区的数据技术进行整合，有助于综合考虑交通与电力、平衡电网、降低电力成本和感受到地方归属感。me^2 促进了城市的需求侧管理，从而改变了消费者对能源的需求——比如在城市社区的高峰时段减少能源使用。

"其中一个动机是将越来越重要的电动汽车和智能电网结合在一起。所有试点项目参与者都安装了智能电表，但我们对电动汽车所能起到的作用尤其感兴趣。参与者不仅有房子，而且还有电动车和充电桩（尤其是在荷兰），有些还有太阳能电池板"，Halldora Thorsdottir 说道。

me^{2}实施的基础之一是家庭和小型企业正在成为小型能源生产商，这有可能成为高峰需求管理和电网平衡的解决方案。75%的荷兰参与者拥有私人充电桩，超过一半的家庭使用太阳能发电装置来生产可再生电力。这一点很重要，因为这些计划和尝试有望成为未来欧盟能源系统管理的一个组成部分。

"这个项目为城市行动者创造了一个新市场，地方电动汽车用户社区和地方智能电表所有者通过城市网络社区聚集在了一起"，项目合作伙伴之一、Moosmoar Energies OG（MME）首席执行官 Wolfgang Prüggler 说道。

（1）里斯本和阿姆斯特丹的试点项目

试点项目旨在测试 me^{2}综合能源监测平台的质量和运行状况。第一个试点项目在里斯本，共50人参加了一个封闭的社区系统。这个项目使用了多个设备来跟踪能源消耗：家庭消耗和充电的智能插头，以及公共充电的 MOBI-E 插头。荷兰的试点项目涉及一个开放系统中的50个家庭，他们均拥有私人电动汽车。这个试点项目与里斯本的并不相同，其电动汽车用户数量更多，这是因为荷兰是欧洲电动汽车占比最高的国家之一。这两个国家的参与者都安装了智能电表，开设了 me^{2}账户（见图13），以便收集他们的能源消耗情况，而他们也可通过个人设备来查看。

图 13　me^2 账户和个人设备

注：通过 me^2 账户和个人设备，消费者可直接获取他们的能源信息，为行为影响机制奠定基础。

（2）游戏化

游戏化是成功的关键。试点之前，跨文化分析清楚表明荷兰的社会性比较和游戏化更为重要，而葡萄牙的参与者不是为了竞争，而是出于自我改善和促进环保的动机。

"两个试点中，我们都鼓励用户减少能源消耗，妥善处理高峰时段的消耗。在葡萄牙，这些主要集中在金融和环境方面。在荷兰，我们侧重的是社会性比较和游戏化。在我们的用户社区，很多人都在尽力做到最好，他们对技术和效率数据非常感兴趣，希望了解自己的表现如何。对于获得的节约回报他们可能不太感兴趣，只是希望能做得更好"，Halldora Thorsdottir 说道。

在葡萄牙，减少能源消耗的用户每周都会获得积分。荷兰的试点项目也引入了一个类似算法，用户在每晚5—9点的高峰时段不仅可获得额外积分，而且还会收到信息"你减少了消耗！"他们还可查看自己的节能排名，获胜者将能获得奖励。项目研究者根据第一阶段的情况发布了一份白皮书报告，针对不同的用户互动阶段提出了建议，同时评估了两个试点城市激励措施的效果以及实际发现。从技术试点获得的一个经验教训是即使这些设备为"即插即用"型，人们也不习惯使用这些设备，大都会说他们明天再用。

这个项目非常复杂，涉及很多方面；它的技术方面非常重要，也很复杂，然后还有开展试点的社会问题，"它需要很长时间才能完全落实，获得最重要的成功因素"，Halldora 一边回顾两年以来的项目情况，一边解释道。

（3）平台和应用程序

me^{2}综合能源监测平台是这个项目智慧城市聚合系统的前端。智慧城市聚合系统将电动汽车电池和家用设备的使用与智能电表连接起来，以在电网或后端实现更高的效率和灵活性。这个系统的前端包括一个社区网站、一个应用程序和一个智能后端。消费者可直接获取他们的能源信息，为行为影响机制奠定基础。应用程序提供 iOS 和 Android 版，有助于增加平台的可及性。用户可以分享自己的成果，比如对所获得的绿色积分，其他用户可以"点赞"。

在智慧城市聚合系统的后端，公用事业公司或各个公司可以收集前端消费者的所有资料。前端已在试点项目中进行了测试，提供了进一步完善的反馈信息。对于能源供应商或可在能源市场进行交易的公司而言，这也可成为一种有趣的产品。Halldora Thorsdottir 认为"你可以优化能源的管理和使用"。

来自智能电表的数据被发送到 me^2 平台。网络平台按照设备、位置或类别（如取暖和制冷）显示消耗情况（见图14）。收集上来的数据会与试点前的调查结果（询问参与者的消耗情况）进行比较。一种用户场景也被开发了出来。技术合作伙伴 MediaPrimer 从一开始就参与了进来，并在前端开发方面付出了很多，如网站、应用程序和平台等。这个聚合系统可通过平台直接与用户通信，并向消费者发送消息，比如"高峰时段为汽车充电代价较高，最好稍后进行"或"另选时段充电将会获得更多积分"。

此外，另一个技术合作伙伴 VPS 还开发出了与平台相连的 me^2 在线市场——市场广场。这背后的想法是有些公司能够提供能效服务，比如有助于电动汽车智能充电的太阳能电池板

图 14　网络平台按照设备、位置或类别（如取暖和

制冷）将消耗情况显示于个人设备

或其他智能工具或服务，它们可作为联营合作伙伴入驻市场广场，而用户可前往查看产品是否诱人。现在已有几个进一步应用成果的想法。

项目的商业合作伙伴现正在思考下一步该怎么走。Halldora Thorsdottir 说："他们希望能进一步推广这个产品，正在积极针对研究、测试和开发展开讨论，然后找到将其推向市场的最佳方式。"

（4）智能电表等智能解决方案何时才能成为标配

"这种情况正在发生。我认为荷兰会有越来越多的人希望了解自己能否节省能源，我们的用户真的希望能在一个地方和平台看到他们所有的生产和消耗情况。这正是 me² 所提供的服务，也是其他智能家居解决方案所要提供的东西，而且有些已经在做了"，Halldora Thorsdottir 对未来前景总结道。

---

me²——智慧城市综合交通和能源平台

持续时间：2016—2018 年

网址：www. jpi-urbaneurope. eu/me2

联系方式：Robert van den Hoed 博士，阿姆斯特丹应用科学大学

电子邮箱：r. van. den. hoed@ hva. nl

合作伙伴：阿姆斯特丹应用科学大学、里斯本天主教大学商业与经济学院、Lisboa E-NOVA、Agência Municipal De Energia-Ambiente De Lisboa、MOOSMOAR Energies、Virtual Power Solutions、MediaPrimer

致谢：该项目已获得欧盟"地平线 2020"研究和创新计划的资助，拨款协议编号为 646453

---

3. 中国案例研究

根据最近的估计，世界城市创造的国内生产总值已占到 80%[①]。同时，它们的能源行业温室气体排放量也达到了全球的 70% 左右；鉴于中国近年来已成为最大的碳排放国，这也

---

① Dobbs，R. 等：《城市世界：描绘城市的经济实力》，2011 年。

给中国城市带来了更多挑战①。

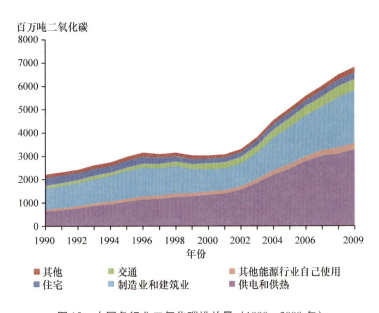

图15　中国各行业二氧化碳排放量（1990—2009 年）

资料来源：经济合作与发展组织、国际能源署，2011 年。

图 15 给出了中国 1990—2009 年各个行业的二氧化碳排放量。根据国际能源署的估算，供电和供热行业的排放量自 1990 年以来大幅增加，已占到 2007 年总排放量的 50% 左右②。

① 世界银行：《中国可持续低碳城市发展》，2012 年。
② 经合组织/国际能源署：《2011 年燃料燃烧二氧化碳排放量》，2009 年。

2013 年，中国排放的二氧化碳占比约为 25%，即 9.2 吉吨；2010—2012 年全球 73% 的碳排放增长发生在中国；如果无法得到遏制，中国的碳排放量可在未来 15 年增加超过 50%[①]。除非采取有效措施来降低碳强度，否则所有关键行业的二氧化碳排放量都会继续快速增长。

幸运的是，政策制定者已在过去几十年认识到节能减排、保持经济强劲增长、创造更多就业机会、提高人们生活质量的必要性。20 世纪 90 年代初，环境保护部以及住房和城乡建设部便开始采取多种措施引导城市实现更可持续的发展，其中包括发布各种生态城市政策和标准。截至 2012 年，环境保护部已命名了 11 个"国家生态市、县、区"，其中包括北京的密云县和延庆县，江苏省的太仓市、张家港市、常熟市和江阴市，山东省的荣成市，深圳的盐田区，上海的闵行区，以及浙江省的安吉县。住房和城乡建设部批准的国家生态园林城市包括深圳、青岛、南京、杭州、威海、扬州、苏州、绍兴、桂林、常熟、昆山和张家港。

除了环境保护部以及住房和城乡建设部之外，国家发改委还于 2010 年启动了全国低碳省区和低碳城市试点工作。这项

---

① Zhu，L.：《中国碳排放报告：2016 年——区域碳排放及其对中国低碳发展的启示》，2016 年。

计划已在全国 5 个省份（广东、辽宁、湖北、陕西、云南）和 8 个城市（天津、重庆、深圳、厦门、杭州、南昌、贵阳和保定）展开实施。

一些地方政府虽然还没有能力建设成为低碳城市，但上述试点项目已对地方政府争取低碳发展的决心产生了积极影响。实践中的一个积极发现是在快速城市化的背景之下，中国城市提高能效和实现低碳发展完全符合城市可持续发展的方向。致力于低碳转型的城市将会变得更宜居、更高效、更具韧性，最终变得更可持续。

深圳、无锡、贵阳、保定和杭州等也提出了低碳城市建设计划，其中一些在性质上与上一代生态城市类似，因此会出现类似的成就和挫折。杭州的低碳城市建设是其中的一个优秀案例。

4. 案例研究——杭州的低碳发展①

浙江省省会杭州市位于中国东部海岸，截至 2016 年年底，其人口为 918.8 万，人口密度每平方千米为 554 人，面积为 16596 平方千米②。它是中国第一个提出低碳城市发展战略的

---

① 参见 http://district.ce.cn/zg/201508/25/t20150825_6311730.shtml；http://hznews.hangzhou.com.cn/jingji/content/2016-10/28/content_6363947.htm；世界银行：《中国可持续低碳城市发展》，2012 年。

② 参见 http://tjj.hangzhou.gov.cn/web/tjnj/nj2017/index.htm。

城市（2008 年），以期到 2015 年将碳强度降低 35％，到 2020 年降低 50％（在 2005 年的基础之上）。

2009 年，杭州发布了《关于建设低碳城市的决定》，旨在将自身转变为低碳城市，成为中国低碳发展的典范。被国家发改委确定为全国首批低碳试点城市之一后，杭州便提出要以低碳经济、低碳建筑、低碳交通、低碳生活、低碳环境、低碳社会为重心，建设低碳示范城市。

从那以后，杭州便采取了各种举措。为了发展低碳经济，它将结构转型和产业升级作为重点，逐步淘汰高污染、高能耗企业，同时鼓励发展清洁生产和循环经济。它还建立了综合性的低碳公交系统，其中包括公共自行车系统、电动出租车服务、低碳公交计划、水上巴士服务和地铁系统。截至 2015 年年底，全市共投入纯电动公交车 1230 辆，纯电动出租车 560辆，CNG（压缩天然气）双燃料出租车 3866 辆，LNG 公交车2378 辆；建成全球规模最大的公共自行车系统，市区已有公共自行车 8 万辆、服务点 3000 多个，累计租用超过 4 亿人次。节能技术已被用于现有和新建建筑，以提高能源效率和减少城市的碳排放，这包括但不限于鼓励发展光伏发电、绿色屋顶和垂直绿化，以及引入绿色建筑评级体系。

杭州采取的以上举措和做法取得了巨大成就。2015 年，杭州市煤炭消费总量比 2012 年下降 6％ 以上，洁净煤使用率达到 80% 以上，可再生能源占能源消费总量的 4% 左右。截至 2015 年，全市单位 GDP 能耗降至 0.43 吨标煤/万元，较 2010 年下降 23.25%，超额完成"十二五"下降 19.5% 的目标。

三　交通出行

1. 概述

全世界都在努力改善交通系统，以帮助公众安全到达公共场所、购买商品、享受服务和经济机会，同时减少交通的环境足迹。解决交通出行问题，会对其他（社会）经济和环境问题以及生活质量和城市人口福祉产生重大影响。在中国和欧洲，人们调查了多模式交通系统和新的出行服务，以解决通勤和拥堵问题。就欧洲的案例研究方面而言，欧洲城市计划项目 Smart Commuting 分析了 3 个国家通勤者的出行行为，以确定新出行服务的需求和潜力。这个项目的结果不仅通过政策制定者得以体现，而且还通过运输公司转化为业务解决方案。上海的案例说明了不同的智能服务将会如何促进多式联运，公共汽车、汽车、火车和自行车都在其中发挥了重要作用。各种交通模式通过创新化应用解决方案连接在了一起，以多模式满足户到户的出行需求。

2. 欧洲案例研究

欧洲城市计划项目：Smart Commuting

Smart Commuting 于 2016 年推出，旨在研究通过智能和可持续的交通系统服务，将工作和生活结合在一起的新方法。这个项目研究了通勤客流，为智能出行服务开发做出了贡献，在努力提高通勤轻松性、灵活性和高效性的同时降低出行成本。它着重研究了奥地利、芬兰和瑞士的 3 个"乘车上班"（Travel-to-Work）区域，以及新型出行概念如何为人们和城市提供支持。

第一个目标是通过调查、访谈和研讨会收集数据，确定移动雇员不断变化的需求。Smart Commuting 能够使用深入浅出的案例研究方法，比较 3 个国家的文化和地理背景。在此背景下，Smart Commuting 会剖析立法、文化和技术政策对选择出行方案的影响。比如，城市在开发公共服务和评估新的基础设施投资时，必须解决通勤问题。

第二个目标是通过新的出行概念和服务，提高交通出行的可持续性。这是由芬兰的按需共享出租车服务合作伙伴 Kyyti 以及奥地利的 ISTmobil 完成的。这个项目有助于评估这些概念如何满足移动雇员不断变化的需求，并从中探寻服务设计和城市规划政策方面的一些共同点。项目合作伙伴 Tuup Oy 的出租车共享系统 Kyyti 已在该项目中获得部分开发。

"项目设计的出发点是让研究活动为实施提供支持。利益攸关方无须等待我们的最终结果，比如，我们已能灵活地在服务开发过程中为公司合作伙伴提供支持"，阿尔托大学的 Matti Vartiainen 教授说道。他一直担任项目负责人，项目经理则是 Teemu Surakka。

在奥地利，出租车共享系统提供商 ISTmobil 为项目研究人员提供了他们服务的使用数据，以评估使用此类系统的好处。由于这些数据源的聚合程度、可及性和完整性均不相同，因此项目整合了不同来源的出行数据来分析出行服务的关键特性。通过数据分析，有助于项目按照用户需求展开更多的服务设计。

由于技术发展、通勤和工作性质等方面的原因，劳动力的流动性会随着时间的推移而增加。但从目前的情况来看，ISTmobil 提供的服务拥有更大潜力，从科尔新堡到维也纳只有 0.06% 的通勤者使用了这项服务。从其他案例来看，芬兰"成长走廊"（Growth Corridor）是首都赫尔辛基附近一个类似的"乘车上班"区域，也可从 ISTmobil 或类似的出行解决方案中受益。项目实施期间，这些服务还扩展到了格拉茨的周边城市，名称为 GUSTmobil。

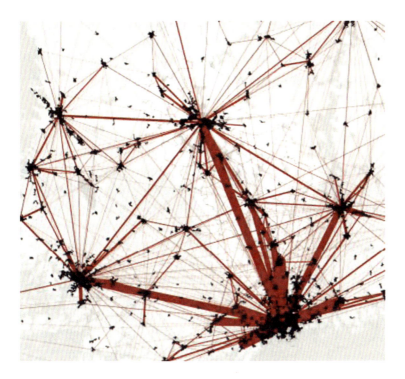

图16　芬兰南部人口中心之间的通勤

资料来源：YKR，2014 年，在 CC BY 4.0 下使用。

　　"我们考虑到了每个国家的制度文化。在芬兰，我们非常注重帮助私营公司开展新服务和进行技术创新；而在瑞士文化中，这些新服务更多被视为公共交通的一种补充，整个行业几乎垄断在两家联邦公司的手中"，Vartiainen 说。他接着说："我们的一项研究结果涉及政策问题：组织这些出行服务需要哪些必要的地方政策？它们的可扩展程度如何？地方环境在很大程度上取决于相关政策的实施。"这个项目还指出了各国在政府结构和交通行业利益攸关方数量方面的差异。

图 17　"通勤基金"（Pendlerfonds）所资助的出行项目

资料来源：Canton of BaselStadt, 2016 年。已获得使用许可。

Smart Commuting 项目收集了移动雇员及其需求的统计数据，比如他们有多少孩子，他们拥有的汽车数量，家庭中的摩托车和电动自行车数量，以及他们的生活环境类型。结果不仅显示了通勤者花费的旅行时间、家庭和工作场所之间的距离，从中还可看出他们对技术系统和不同应用程序的使用方式、上下班途中所做的事情以及选择某种交通方式的缘由。

"我认为我们已获得了各种各样的结果，但最重要的是对 3 个国家进行了用户调查——比较每个国家的出行情况和交通需求，以及用户认为新的出行方案能否满足需求"，Vartiainen 说。

"我们已掌握了很多交通参与者方面的见解，了解了各国在服务提供和使用方面的差异。我们还受邀在"欧盟城市议程"政策实验室讨论我们的研究结果，这表明人们需要这些见解和政策思路"，Teemu Surakka 说。

这个项目为通勤系统规划、服务设计以及城市和区域规划积累了新知识，并使人们明白了确立出行系统和解决方案时应该考虑的重要因素。对于相关公司而言，这不仅意味着服务内容的联合开发，而且还会产生直接的商业效应——Tuup Oy 已在项目中开始与 Swiss PostBus 展开合作。

"这是加入财团的驱动因素之一。现在，我们已开始为瑞士的 Kyyti 建立类似的服务。它已测试使用了几个月，将会在苏黎世郊外的布鲁格推出"，Tuup/Kyyti 的 Johanna Taskinen 说。Tuup Oy 还将与一家公司客户合作展开一个新项目，在奥卢市有组织地测试他们的解决方案。Taskinen 女士认为这个项目是持续推进产品开发的一个环节。

这项研究还分析了交通新模式的市场潜力，如共享汽车、按需服务和共享单车，以及通勤者希望看到的推动因素——更多的笔记本电脑放置空间、更好的互联网连接、安静的工作空间和允许在路上办公。这些发现都为下一个 Smart Commuting 项目奠定了基础。

"我们已与类似的合作伙伴提交了一份'地平线 2020'提案，但现在的城市合作伙伴都面临着可持续通勤方面的挑战。我们能够证明可为城市提供最好的政策和工具，这是主要的收获。我很高兴能参与这个项目并展开合作"，Matti Vartiainen 总结道。

Smart Commuting——增长地区的智慧出行

持续时间：2016—2018 年

网址：https：//smartcommuting. eu/

联系方式：Matti Vartiainen 教授，阿尔托大学

电子邮箱：matti. vartiainen@ aalto. fi

合作伙伴：阿尔托大学、奥地利科技学院、tbw research GesmbH、苏黎世应用

科学大学、Virta 有限公司（Liikennevirta 公司）、AC2SG 软件公司、Tuup 公司、ISTmobil 公司、芬兰"成长走廊"、巴塞尔城市州交通出行办公室

致谢：该项目已获得欧盟"地平线 2020"研究和创新计划的资助，拨款协议编号为 646453

3. 中国案例研究

城市公共交通是城市可持续发展的关键组成部分，它所提供的交通出行方式比私家车更节能[1]。因此，与以汽车为导向的发展模式相比，以公共交通为导向有助于减少碳排放，从而促进可持续发展。图 18 的示例表明，公共汽车或地铁系统在高峰时段的能源消耗和温室气体排放比私家车更少（每乘客公里的生命周期排放量）[2]。

为了缓解交通拥堵，中国的一些城市已开始仿照上海和北京，从交通需求的角度采取了一些措施（如新车限购，收取和提高停车费）[3]。这些措施再加上地铁系统和快速公交系统

---

[1]　世界银行：《中国可持续低碳城市发展》，2012 年。

[2]　Chester and Horvath, "Environmental Assessment of Passenger Transportation should Include Infrastructure and Supply Chains", *Environmental Research Letters*, 4, 2009, pp. 1 – 8.

[3]　Wang, J. and He, D., "Sustainable Urban Development in China: Challenges and Achievements", *Mitigation and Adaptation Strategies for Global Change*, 20, 2015, pp. 665 – 682.

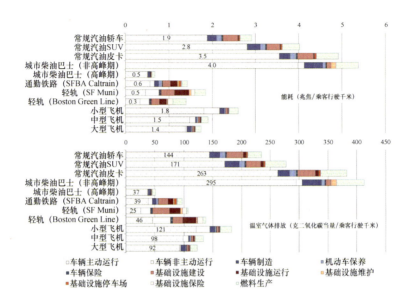

图18　每乘客千米的生命周期排放量

注：对于每个乘客行驶千米（PKT）的能耗和温室气体排放，车辆运行组件以灰色图案显示，其他车辆组件以蓝色阴影显示，基础设施组件以红色和橙色显示，燃料生产组件以绿色显示，所有组件的显示顺序与图例一致。

资料来源：Chester 和 Horvath，2009 年。

（如广州）等公共交通系统的进一步发展，促进了公共交通乘客的增多和私家车使用的减少。从某种程度来说，这些变化进一步缓解了这些城市的交通拥堵，但要实现大幅削减仍有很长的路要走。以下是上海的智能交通出行优秀案例。

4. 案例研究——上海智能交通出行①

2010 年举办世博会之后，上海的智能交通出行开始加速发展。从那时起，智能交通技术已被广泛应用于交通运输领域，比如轨道交通、公共汽车和无轨电车、公共停车场和交通枢纽，这些都有助于促进交通管理和与公众共享信息。

为了提供一站式的交通信息平台，上海市交通委员会还发布了"上海交通"应用程序。这款应用程序包括 12 个功能模块（见图 19），涵盖了空中、水上和陆地交通状况，能够实时提供公交、地铁、道路状况及渡轮、机场巴士等方面的信息。它能帮助居民规划门到门的步行、公共交通和驾车行程。居民还可查看公交卡和 ETC 卡中的余额，并查找电动汽车充电位置的信息。

上海还有其他深受欢迎的交通应用，比如"上海公交"和"上海地铁"，专门提供公共汽车、快速交通、高速公路以及地铁服务的信息。上海实现以上所述的智能交通出行，离不开强大的硬件和软件支持以及实时数据馈送。比如，通过"上海公交"应用便可访问该市 648 条公交线路的数据。上海巴士公交（集团）有限公司能在考虑路线规划、道路状况、公

---

① http://www.sohu.com/a/198740991_182825；http://www.shanghai.gov.cn/nw2/nw2314/nw2315/nw4411/u21aw1236157.html；http://www.shanghai.gov.cn/nw2/nw2314/nw2315/nw4411/u21aw1283651.html.

图 19　"上海交通"应用

资料来源：苹果商店。

交车位置的基础之上计算出最佳的公交出发和到达时间，实现智能调度。到目前为止，浦东区已有近 4000 辆公交车加入了智能调度系统，覆盖 340 多条公交线路。

上述公共交通工具和上海的共享单车为解决"最后一千米"问题做出了巨大贡献，人们可骑车从公共交通站点到达目的地。从图 20 可看出，2016 年上海 90% 的共享单车活跃在公交站点周边，51% 活跃在地铁站点周边①。值得注意的是，这些数据的收集范围是公交站点 300 米以内、地铁站点 500 米以内的区域，这两个区域之间存在一些重叠。有关共享单车的案例研究将在下面进行单独论述。

图 20　2016 年上海和北京公共交通与共享单车系统的搭配使用情况

资料来源：清华同衡规划设计研究院和摩拜单车：《2017 年共享单车与城市发展白皮书》，2017 年。

---

① 清华同衡规划设计研究院和摩拜单车：《2017 年共享单车与城市发展白皮书》，2017 年。

四 共享经济

1. 概述

随着数字技术的发展，共享经济已成为现实。城市人口越来越喜欢共享而不是拥有，共享服务正在从社会、环境和经济方面影响城市生活。共享经济提供了挑战常规的潜力。在欧洲和中国，新的共享计划正在深刻影响城市生活和消费模式，并可为城市可持续发展做出重大贡献。欧洲城市计划项目 E4 - shares 开发出了灵活、高效和经济可行的电动汽车共享系统模型。该项目以维也纳为例，比较了不同的汽车共享模型，制定了用户激励机制，并研究了支持性政策框架。在中国，共享经济最近获得了长足发展。2015 年以来，新的共享计划和商业模式进一步助推了中国的自行车共享热潮。现如今，自行车共享对于解决"最后一千米"问题（公共交通与人们最终目的地之间的距离）发挥了重要作用。

2. 欧洲案例研究

欧洲城市计划项目：E4 - share

E4 - share 项目为灵活、高效和经济可行的电动汽车共享系统奠定了基础，市民能够有效地使用和转换不同的交通方式。实施这个项目的目的是为电动汽车共享系统开发通用模型，以供欧洲各个城市应用，并研究和解决设计和运作中的优化问题。

人们越来越关注城市不可持续交通系统方面的问题，其中包括拥堵、空气污染和噪音，以及它们对市民健康和生活质量的影响。城市正面临严峻挑战，需要一个转型过程来减轻污染、减少能源和土地消耗，同时提高市民可用公共空间的质量。优化城市的交通系统是改善城市交通系统的一项中心任务。

共享汽车是所谓"共享经济"——分享商品和服务——的组成部分（《经济学家》，2013 年），比如租赁而不是购买汽车。用户可选择汽车车型（大型或小型）、驱动方式（燃油或电动）和取还方式（自由流动或定点取还）。汽车共享系统越来越受欢迎，过去几年全球运营公司的数量都在增加。同时，一些运营商已退出市场，表明它们缺乏可持续的商业模式。在共享经济的专题领域和私营部门的贡献方面，这个项目为运营商的用户激励机制提出了宝贵见解，并提供了新兴市场优化技术和商业模式的工具。

E4 – share 是一个由欧洲城市计划试点二期资助的国际研究项目，旨在开发"生态、经济、高效的电动汽车共享模型"。这个项目已于 2017 年结束，由维也纳大学、奥地利科技学院、tbw research（一家从事研究和创新项目的非营利组织）、布鲁塞尔自由大学、博洛尼亚大学与共享汽车运营商合作实施。

（1）维也纳案例研究

维也纳是一个开展案例研究的城市。研究者将这个城市划分为不同的运营区域，并利用出租车数据进行了需求假设。额外的投入包括共享汽车运营商固定的投资预算，汽车共享用户的最长步行距离为 5 分钟。维也纳模型的目的在于优化预期销售额、地点设置和激励措施，建立平衡的车辆和车站模型。

维也纳案例中开发的建模、优化和模拟方法具有可借鉴性和可扩展性，因此也适用于其他城市和应用场景（比如共享单车、公共场所的充电站）。

共享汽车服务基本存在两种类型：定点取还式——汽车使用者在城市的固定地点取还汽车；自由流动式——汽车几乎可停放在城市的任何地方。自由流动式是趋势所在，用户最喜欢这种服务。这个项目开发的数学模型应适用于上述两种共享汽车服务，因此必须解决很多问题。定点取还式系统的问题可能包括：在哪里建设取还站？每个站点应设多少充电桩？可为哪些客户提供服务？所有这些问题都已得到解决。另外，自由流动式系统不仅需要有效布局充电站，而且还需开发激励策略或激励系统，尽可能提高车辆维护、充电和其他必要维修工作的

图21　电动汽车共享系统热图

注：颜色越暗表示该路段更常使用（奥地利科技学院）。

效率。

（2）深入探索用户激励措施

这个项目深入探索了哪些激励措施才能有效减轻车队管理负担，为共享汽车运营商提供优化运营的新方法。

为了分析现有的激励措施——尤其是未来潜在的激励措施，以及可由用户接管的潜在管理任务，项目不仅详细研究了现有的共享汽车运营商，而且还举办了研讨会，进行了在线调查。各种因素被相互关联在了一起，比如收入、共享汽车使用行为、对潜在激励措施的兴趣以及金额。这些结果被整合进了数学模型，通过用户激励目录呈现了出来。

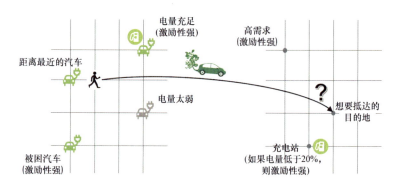

图 22　用户激励

（3）共享汽车运营商解决方案示例

E4‐share 项目为共享汽车位置规划和充电站提供了一种示例方案，并对车辆使用强度、系统中的车辆取还、不同规模运作区域的系统效率进行了大量评估和分析。这些解决方案可为运营商提供决策支持，帮助他们应对关键的战略、战术和运营问题。使用电动汽车而不是燃油汽车为改善城市生活质量提供了机会，但同时也对服务提供商和城市管理部门形成了特定挑战。

根据维也纳案例开发的模型通常适用于各种规划层面的规

划及运作优化。根据这些复杂数学模型进行的模拟，以及使用站点、客户请求和步行范围构建的简化网络可参见项目网站①。

（4）为城市决策者确定了机会

这个项目的成果为实施市场监管、更好地利用技术解决方案，以及构建高效和可持续的城市系统和网络提供了支撑。

"目前，维也纳并未对共享汽车市场和运营商进行规范，"tbw research 项目负责人 Marlene Hawelka 说，"但共享出行服务能够成为城市交通的一种宝贵资产和公共交通的一种补充，有助于减少交通系统的土地消耗。因此，我们还需进一步扩展汽车共享系统，将外城区的市民也纳入该系统。在当今未经规范的市场上，共享汽车运营商主要是在城市中心提供服务，但在那里你也可选择步行和搭乘电车。"

此外，数字平台和 MaaS（出行即服务）还能将新服务无缝集成到现有的城市交通系统中。

E4 – share——生态、经济、高效的电动汽车共享模型

持续时间：2014—2017 年

网址：www. univie. ac. at/e4 – share

联系方式：Markus Leitner，维也纳大学

电子邮箱：markus. leitner@ univie. ac. at

---

① http：//www. univie. ac. at/e4 – share/.

合作伙伴：奥地利科技学院、布鲁塞尔自由大学、博洛尼亚大学、tbw research GesmbH、维也纳大学

3. 中国案例研究

共享经济在过去 10 年获得快速发展，是追求更好的价值再分配和协同消费以及国际金融危机后自然资源约束日益突出的结果①。在线点对点（P2P）分享未被充分利用的商品和服务，有助于减少生态足迹②。因此，共享经济可能成为实现可持续发展的一种新途径③。

近年来，世界见证了共享经济的繁荣发展，中国的共享经济也是如此④。根据国家信息中心分享经济研究中心发布的

---

① https：//www. ted. com/talks/lisa_ gansky_ the_ future_ of_ business_ is_ the_ mesh；https：//www. youtube. com/watch? v = AQa3kUJPEko；Schor, J. and Fitzmaurice, C. , "Collaborating and Connecting：The Emergence of the Sharing Economy", in *Handbook on Research on Sustainable Consumption*, eds. , Lucia Reisch and John Thogersen, 2015, Cheltenham, UK：Edward Elgar；McLaren, D. and Agyeman, J. , *Sharing Cities：A Case for Truly Smart and Sustainable Cities*, 2015, Cambridge, Massachusetts：The MIT Press。

② Cheng, M. :《共享经济：未来研究的回顾与议程》，《国际营销管理杂志》2016 年第 57 期。

③ Heinrichs, H. , "Sharing Economy：A Potential New Pathway to Sustainability", *Gaia*, 22（4）, 2013, pp. 228 – 231.

④ 翁士洪:《城市共享单车监管体制的整体治理创新研究》，《电子政务》2018 年第 4 期。

《中国共享经济发展年度报告（2017）》，共享经济是指"利用互联网等现代信息技术，以使用权分享为主要特征，整合海量、分散化资源，满足多样化需求的经济活动总和"。根据《中国共享经济发展年度报告（2018）》①，2017 年中国共享经济交易额为 49205 亿元，比 2016 年增长 47.2%。超过 7 亿人参与了共享经济，与 2016 年相比增加约 1 亿人。

图 23 显示了中国 2017 年共享经济的交易额增长率（按行业划分）。7 个关键领域中，知识技能（126.6%）、生活服务（82.7%）和房屋（70.6%）的增长率排在前三。据估计，未来 5 年共享经济的年均增长率将保持在 30% 以上。

共享经济的快速发展可能与中国城市的低碳发展没有直接关系，这可能取决于各个领域的性质以及它们与减少生态足迹的关系。比如，交通出行领域的单车和汽车共享有助于降低汽车使用水平，从而对低碳和可持续发展产生积极影响；但在生活服务领域，一些提供过度包装商品的服务可能就不是这样。以下是中国共享单车方面的案例研究。不可否认，共享单车可能存在财务可持续性和城市管理等潜在问题，本案例研究的重点是中国共享单车与城市可持续发展之间的关系。

---

① http：//tech.ifeng.com/a/20180228/44890942_0.shtml；http：//baijiahao.baidu.com/s？id=1594089458520055061&wfr=spider&for=pc.

图 23　中国 2017 年共享经济交易额增长率（按行业划分）（％）

资料来源：根据《中国共享经济发展年度报告（2018）》数据编制。

4. 案例研究——中国共享单车

近年来，中国出现了共享单车热潮，数字创新在其中发挥了关键作用。如前文所述，共享单车的目的是解决"最后一英里"的问题，人们可骑车从公共交通站点到达目的地。共享单车是共享经济中的一种商业新模式：企业与地方政府合作，在公共场所、住宅区、商业区、公交车站和地铁站等场所之内或周围提供自行车租赁服务①。

——————————

①　翁士洪：《城市共享单车监管体制的整体治理创新研究》，《电子政务》2018 年第 4 期。

在中国，共享单车也是公共自行车共享所获得的最新发展。随着创新技术的发展，这个事物存在两个发展阶段。第一阶段始于 2008 年，公共自行车的概念被引入中国市场，其中包括公共自行车和泊位。"杭州公共自行车"是中国公共自行车共享方面一个极好的例子。2008 年，由于交通拥堵和环境问题日益严重，杭州市政府启动了"杭州公共自行车"项目，为全市公共交通提供无缝支线服务。项目最初启动时共有 2800 辆自行车，30 个固定泊位和 30 个移动泊位（可根据需要进行移动）（见图 24）[1]；截至 2013 年 1 月 5 日，它已发展成为全球最大的公共自行车共享系统，拥有自行车 66500 辆，站点 2700 个，为城市减少碳排放做出了巨大贡献[2]。

随着创新技术的发展，2015 年以来无桩共享单车在中国迅速扩张。在中国，共享单车和公共自行车共享之间，以及共享单车初创公司之间展开了激烈竞争。最终，摩拜单车和小黄车从众多共享单车初创公司脱颖而出，占据了最大市场份额。无桩共享单车配备了 GPS 及其他创新技术，能够从自行车使

---

[1]　Shaheen, S. , Zhang, H. , Martin, E. and Guzman, S. , *Transportation Research Record*: *Journal of the Transportation Research Board*, 2247, 2011, pp. 33 – 41.

[2]　https://web. archive. org/web/20140808045713/; http://www.zj. xinhua-net. com/newscenter/focus/2013 – 01/05/c_ 114258328. htm.

图 24　杭州公共自行车

资料来源：http：//policytransfer. metropolis. org/case-studies/hangzhou-china-urban-public-bicycle-sharing-program。

用中收集大量数据，继而通过优化算法实现智能调度①。

　　共享单车热潮为居民提供了一种"智能"城市短途出行的替代方案，对低碳和城市可持续发展具有推动作用。根据清华同衡规划设计研究院和摩拜单车发布的《2017 年共享单车与城市发展白皮书》②，自 2015 年引入共享单车以来，2016 年自行车在最受欢迎的城市交通方式（即小汽车、公共汽车、地铁和自行车）中的占比已增加 6.1%（从 5.5% 增至

---

　　①　翁士洪：《城市共享单车监管体制的整体治理创新研究》，《电子政务》2018 年第 4 期。

　　②　http：//www. fietsberaad. nl/？ lang = en&repository = White + paper + 2017 + Bike-sharing + and + the + City.

11.6%）。全国骑行总距离已达 25 亿公里，减少碳排放量 54
万吨（见图 25）。共享单车在一定程度上减少了对汽车的依
赖，同一时期，开车出行在最受欢迎的城市交通方式中的占比
下降了 3.2%（从 29.8% 降至 26.6%）。

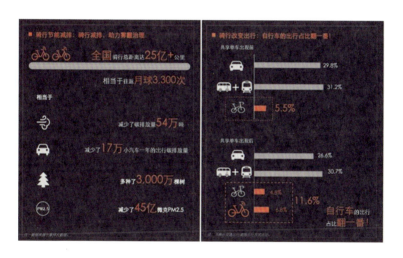

图 25　共享单车改变了城市出行方式并促进减少碳排放

资料来源：清华同衡规划设计研究院和摩拜单车：《2017 年共享单车与城市
发展白皮书》，2017 年。

五　智慧城市治理

1. 概述

为有效制定和实施城市可持续发展战略，私人和公共利益

攸关方需展开新的治理合作，使能技术、大数据和"实时"行动为创新和智慧城市治理与管理提供新的途径。如今，人们很容易找到多种信息进行城市决策，但需要适当的工具和方法来巩固和集成。欧洲城市计划项目 UrbanData2Decide 旨在利用公共社交媒体和开放数据库的信息，为城市治理开发决策支持系统。与此同时，数字技术和社交媒体也为参与式规划和治理提供了支持。另一个欧洲城市计划项目公共空间孵化器在参与式规划过程中嵌入了这些新技术，以便所有利益攸关方都可为城市规划做出贡献。该项目在伦敦、布鲁塞尔和都灵设立了城市创新应用实验室。在中国，许多城市都推出了电子政务服务。中国已有 80 个城市开展了"信息惠民"试点项目，建立电子政务在线服务平台。威海的智慧城市治理旨在促进制度变革、公共行政能力建设和社会技术创新，继而挖掘智能技术的潜力。

2. 欧洲案例研究

欧洲城市计划项目：UrbanData2Decide

UrbanData2Decide 项目旨在从公共社交媒体和开放数据库这两个来源提取和处理信息。其目的在于开发新方法，将现有的大数据库和专家知识融入一个优化框架，从而为城市管理的整体决策提供支持。

市政当局每天都需做出数百项决策，城市决策者如今面临的挑战前所未有，但也存在新的机遇；周围的环境变得越来越复杂。但迄今为止，对决策具有重要意义的消息来源还基本处在尚未开发的阶段。UrbanData2Decide 希望能从不断增加的数据量中探寻出答案。

UrbanData2Decide 启动于 2014 年①，力求创建数字时代做出反应和决策所需的工具。它综合考虑了从社交媒体和开放数据源提取和处理的信息以及专家小组的建议，在考虑所有利益攸关方的观点和意见的基础上为地方政府迈向全面、可持续和有理有据的决策过程提供支持。所面临的挑战包括如何更好地控制数据、扩充可用数据、提高对开放数据和其他数据源所具有的积极影响的认识。在实践中，这个过程包括收集数据、分析数据以及对数据进行可视化处理。维也纳市进行的案例研究通过 10 个例子，分析了如何利用 UrbanData2Decide 决策支持工具来对当前和未来的项目提供指导。

（1）UrbanData2Decide 的结构

该项目的实施背景可分为三个子组：域、利益攸关方和空间层面，除此之外还有数据伦理、所需数据和访问类型。经过可视化，创建了一系列以简单易懂的方式显示数据的方法。

---

① http：//www. urbandata2decide. eu/wp-content/uploads/deliverables/Urban Data2Decide-D1. 1-Kick-off-Meeting-Report. pdf.

UrbanData2Decide 的最后一部分是决策的关键目标：行动者、方法、专家参与和技术解决方案；此外，频率、水平和持续时间也是这个过程的要素。

我们可以看到在城市背景中使用"数据科学"进行知情决策正在成为一种趋势，而我们的研究符合这一方向。牛津大学牛津互联网研究所高级研究员 Jonathan Bright 博士说："理想结果是我们能向政策制定者提供更好的数据，帮助他们做出更好的决策。"

项目负责方 SYNYO 专注于研究和设计新型的信息通信技术解决方案，进行数据分析和使信息可视化。SYNYO 的重点是态势感知（了解城市状况），研究所遇问题的解决方案，并选择其中一些进行开发：趋势监测（对社交媒体和报纸、博客等在线媒体进行文本分析）、可视化监测（图像、视频）、组织流（社会流）和开放数据地图。哥本哈根大学的工作重点是图片，尤其是来自 Instagram 的图片。

哥本哈根市希望向公众提供数据，促使公民更好地了解情况和展开对话，因此也参与了这个项目。哥本哈根市进行的案例研究侧重于市政空间规划，其中包括如何与公民合作，以做出长期决策。

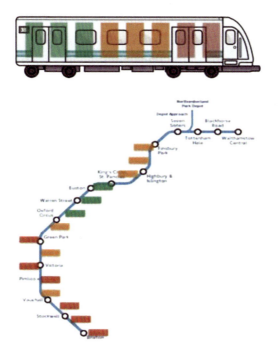

图26 伦敦地铁拥挤指示图

　　有关如何使用这些城市数据的另一个例子，是开放数据研究所为伦敦地铁公司（goingunderground. herokuapp. com）制作的列车信号数据演示器。随着时间变化的列车数据通过信号图形展示出来，由此可在多个传感器数据集之间展开比较。这些数据是对维多利亚线上特定时间和特定车站，即将到站列车的占用率进行可视化的基础。

图27　预测和管理城市复杂问题的综合数据可视化和决策解决方案

（2）UrbanDataVisualiser 和 UrbanDecisionMaker[①]

根据广泛收集而来的社交媒体内容和开放数据集，Urban-DataVisualiser 将能使用一种多层次、多维度的方法对这些数据进行聚合、构建和可视化处理。这个框架广泛使用了数据挖掘、情感分析和可视化技术，最终开发出一种概念验证演示器，将信息直观和清晰地展示出来。为了开发 UrbanDataVisualiser，他们还编写了一份各国不同工具的报告，分析了不同的数据监测和可视化方式以及对不同数据源的使用，概述了所使用的工具和来源。在这里，这个项目还概述了不同的数据类型以及各类数据的可及性[②]。开放数据研究所开发出了可视化工具和应用示例。

① http：//www.urbandata2decide.eu/wp-content/uploads/deliverables/Urban Data2Decide-D3.1-UrbanDataVisualiser-Report.pdf.

② Ibid..

他们开发出了不同的可视化途径和方法，供使用方使用。"你会发现可使用不同的可视化形式来轻松理解大批量的数据，"马尔默大学的 Per-Olof Hallin 说道，他是这个项目的一位参与者。

另外，UrbanDecisionMaker 工具能够利用科学的多轮专家集成方法和工具（比如 Delphi）对外部专家和顾问进行整合，这项结构化沟通技术是一种基于专家小组的系统性和交互式预测方法，其中包含有 Expert Integrator、Collective Deliberation Tool 和 Expert Pool 等工具[①]。

UrbanData2Decide 的结果显示出了开发可视化工具的必要性，该项目已能测试数个原型。这些测试结果已被用于城市安全和安保等项目。

案例中的结果没有使用数据，没有解决这个问题的政策，也没有好的方法。"这部分是因为人们不习惯使用这些数据源，而且行动者比较杂乱，"Per-Olof Hallin 说。

该研究正处在试验阶段，许多城市正在尝试使用数据解决大量不同的问题；建议在机构层面开放这类实验，以便员工处理、获取和应用数据，并尝试开发有用的工具。"这种'初

[①] http：//www. urbandata2decide. eu/wp-content/uploads/deliverables/Urban Data2Decide-D3. 3-Interface-Design. pdf.

创'文化历来难在地方政府背景下发展（至少英国如此），它们的预算非常紧张，人们非常害怕失败，"Jonathan Bright 针对其他人的建议评论道。

UrbanData2Decide 在开发数据收集和共享方法时也为其他项目提供了灵感，比如联合概述不同利益攸关方（比如政府部门和私营企业，市议会和业主）之间的情况。UrbanData2Decide 一直致力于创建教学过程，探寻将数据用于城市开发的共同观点。

UrbanData2Decide——预测和管理城市复杂问题的综合数据可视化和决策解决方案

持续时间：2014—2016 年

网址：www.urbandata2decide.eu

联系方式：Peter Leitner

电子邮箱：peter.leitner@synyo.com

合作伙伴：牛津大学、牛津互联网研究所、马尔默大学、开放数据研究所、哥本哈根信息技术大学、软件开发小组、社会创新中心（ZSI）、SYNYO 公司、研发部

欧洲城市计划项目：公共空间孵化器

公共空间孵化器项目能够提供一些工具和手段，促使地方利益攸关方积极参与旨在塑造地方环境的活动。该项目致力于

利用新技术的力量，将其整合入共创性城市规划和治理当中，其中包括多个利益攸关方共同打造充满活力的公共空间。公共空间孵化器允许地方利益攸关方通过网络或参加公共会议，使用简单明了的 3D 空间模型轻松塑造他们自己的地方场景。他们可以四处漫步或在环境中自由飞翔，改变自己所处的环境，不断探索和修改。然后，他们会对场景进行众筹，作为提供自己支持的方案。

（1）将新技术嵌入参与式规划过程

从人工智能到在线网站界面的新技术发展——城市功能和可视化开发建议的"仪表板"——为建成环境用户释放了巨大潜力，他们能在解释和主动塑造自己的建成环境方面发挥更积极的作用。这些发展不仅为人机交互的设计和管理带来了技术挑战，而且还提出了这样的疑问：这些技术挑战为何与不同类型用户的能力和倾向密切相关？因此，他们提出了"谁最能充分利用这些技术过程？""他们怎样才能更好地嵌入特定的参与式规划过程？"等问题。

（2）在线平台和场景

公共空间孵化器是一项由欧洲城市计划试点二期资助的国际研究项目，它设计宏伟，由都灵理工大学牵头实施，合作伙伴包括 Innovation Service Network 公司、天主教鲁汶大学、Neurovation 公司、伦敦大学学院和都灵市。

　　该项目旨在为空间和社区的自我组织提供支持，通过多种途径激励、鼓励和促使城市行动者达成共识。这将需要合理的论证、共识和合作来打造协调行动的空间，而不是简单地依靠自上而下的战略思维。实现这一目标的手段是信息和通信技术，借助于它们行动者将能提升自己的城市空间共创能力。

图 28　案例研究方案示例

　　为此，这个项目开发并应用了一个在线平台。公共用户可通过这个在线平台访问站点信息，通过远程并以交互的方式为城市结构干预提出创新建议（比如添加一条长凳甚至整个公园，或随便移动现有元素），这一切都通过 3D 场景实现了可视化。场景能对可灵活定制和按需实施的各种规模和预算干预进行连贯概述，从而使社区能够控制自己的进程，"塑造"自己的空间。

这个项目的关键部分是开发一种系统，即一种分类体系，利用相关概念、要素及相互关系将有关城市空间领域的知识从概念上转化为一种具有分层结构和相互关联的语义结构，从而提供明确和无法混淆的定义。

（3）构想众包和项目众筹

开放式创新和大众技术是这个项目的另一个特色。过去几年间，众筹已成为一种颇具前途的工具，不仅能为私人项目、公共组织或初创企业筹集资金，而且也可为城市地区筹集资金。除了获取财务资源外，与大众相关的活动还能在创新和风险管理方面提供多种附加值。

这个项目还为众包和众筹空间创造开发了一个软件平台，大众可在整个创新过程中邀请广大目标群体针对特定挑战提出他们的构想、针对项目构想提供反馈或投票选出最佳构想，从而实现构想的众包（见图29）。成功通过第一阶段评估的设想会在适当的众筹平台获得进一步的推广支持。因此，新的合作开发项目的诞生，依靠的是相关知识的众筹和资金的筹措。

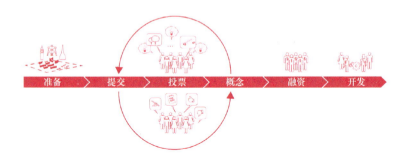

图29　众创和众筹过程概述

（4）伦敦、布鲁塞尔和都灵的城市创新应用实验室

这个项目的方法和技术已通过三个城市的城市创新应用实验室进行了测试，每个创新应用实验室都有机会展示自己特定和基于背景的配置，为地方空间的自我组织提供最佳支持。

伦敦的案例研究使用了一块14公顷的现有住宅区波拉德山（Pollards Hill）。布鲁塞尔创新应用实验室位于约萨法特（Josaphat），覆盖面积30公顷，目前正计划改造成为一个新的可持续社区。约萨法特的案例非常有趣，实验了如何利用孵化器工具为该地当前和未来的使用提供支持，满足市民和公共利益攸关方的愿望。

都灵创新应用实验室主要研究如何重建 Quartiere Mirafiori Sud，这个由高层公寓组成的公益社区建于20世纪60年代中期，共含2700套住宅和6000名居民。通过研讨会以及创新应用实验室的其他活动，地方利益攸关方参与了协作和自我组织场景的定义，以期修复公共空间和建筑。

（5）数字平台已做好应用准备

布鲁塞尔、伦敦和都灵的公共空间孵化器项目经验很有前途。"分类体系似乎能够引发讨论，并有助于阐明观点。事实证明，利益攸关方利用 3D 模型塑造自己的场景是一种很有前景的方法，它有助于增强非专业人士之间的理解，从而为塑造地方社区做出更大贡献。"意大利都灵理工大学研究员 Luca Caneparo 说道："测试设计平台和对象分类，有助于洞察利益攸关方在理解地图对象方面的差异。各国之间存在差异，便需按照不同国家的需求对工具进行定制和调整。"

大体而言，数字平台已可从试点案例迈入推广阶段，将其用于社区层面的其他项目；但目前，合法产权是这个工具进一步应用的障碍。

公共空间孵化器

持续时间：2014—2017 年

网址：www. jpi-urbaneurope. eu/incubators

联系方式：Luca Caneparo，都灵理工大学

电子邮箱：luca. caneparo@ polito. it

合作伙伴：Innovation Service Network 公司、天主教鲁汶大学、Neurovation 公司、伦敦大学学院、都灵市、都灵理工大学

---

3. 中国案例研究

与智慧城市的概念类似，智慧城市治理也存在多种概念。不过，人们普遍认为智慧城市治理不只是一个技术问题，因为技术本身不可能让城市变得更加智能；培育智慧城市需要从政治层面理解技术。因此，智慧城市治理是一个涉及制度变革的复杂过程，需要进行社会技术治理，并利用信息通信技术创造人类合作的新形式，从而实现更好的结果和更开放的治理①。过去几十年来，社会结构与新技术之间的协同作用一直是电子政务研究的核心，尤其是分析如何利用新技术来提高政府质量和效力②。

过去几年间，中国利用更先进的信息和网络技术，已在智慧城市治理方面取得了进步和制度方面的突破。"互联网＋"深度改变了城市管理模式以及服务提供和交付方式。更加智能的人口管理、检测城市道路网络、智能应急响应系统是智慧城市治理的典型例子。

到目前为止，中国已有80个城市开展了"信息惠民"试

---

① Meijer, A. and Bolívar, M, "Governing the Smart City: A Review of the Literature on Smart Urban Governance", *International Review of Administrative Sciences*, 82（2）, 2016, pp. 392 – 408.

② Gil-Garcia R., *Enacting Electronic Government Success: An Integrative Study of Government-wide Websites, Organizational Capabilities, and Institutions*, 2012, New York: Springer.

点项目。电子政务提高了政府效率。山东、浙江和广东通过引入在线服务平台，进一步创新和改善了城市的政府服务、透明运作和执法监督。

4. 案例研究——威海智慧城市治理①

威海自 2013 年开始建设智慧城市，四大目标中有三个与智慧城市治理密切相关，即完善信息基础设施、提高治理能力、通过加强公共服务的提供与管理改善民生（第四个是刺激城市经济发展）。威海从那时起已实施了多个项目。以下是与智慧城市治理相关的主要措施和成就。

（1）整合部门资源，实行电子政务。该市投资 1350 万元建立了基于云计算的电子政务系统，为政府部门安装了 98 条光纤，集成了 150 多个计算机簇和服务器设备；已在 200 多个政府部门实现了统一技术平台、计算和存储、集成式内外网络以及统一的安保、运行和维护。

（2）利用电子政务改善治理和公共服务提供。该市已建立综合网络系统，以提高治理和公共服务提供的成效和效率。这个系统包括一个公共服务提供和信息共享门户网站②，公民可通过个人电脑、手机、平板电脑和数字电视进行访问，以及

① http://www.wheitc.gov.cn/art/2018/3/14/art_ 6864_ 1163457. html.

② http://www.whsmwy.com/wh_ portal/.

提供智能社区、医疗保健、教育、交通出行、旅游和文化服务的多功能市民卡。

（3）引入智能交通管理，减少拥塞。该市已建成智能管控平台和8个应用系统，整合和实时监控路况、事件、天气等情况，自动识别重点车辆并报警，每5分钟发布重点路口路段信息，由此减少了中心城区工作日早晚高峰时段的路网平均车速。

（4）智慧城市建设档案。该档案包括地下管线信息系统、城建档案归档系统、勘察现场数据采集和建设项目流程数据采集系统；已挂接73个工程的967卷档案，覆盖给水、排水、燃气、热力、电力、电信6个垂直行业，共计13994千米管线数据96G。

（5）智慧水务、供热和供电管理。该市已建成供水管线数字化平台和供排水调度指挥系统，与热电、通信、燃气等管线实现信息共享，提供现场数据实时采集、自动报警、应急指挥调度等功能。此外，它还建成了智能供电平台，131万客户实现用电信息自动采集和电费自动核算；开展了光伏储能微网、光导照明、节能路灯、智能用电控制、充电桩、居民家庭能效服务六位一体的智能供电服务。此外，该市还建立了智能供热管理平台，完成改造安装楼道智能电动调节阀12880个，安装户内温控阀33万个，由此降低能耗27.6%，实现了热计量数字化、节能监测智能化和政府监管网络化。

第四章　结论

　　结论部分旨在通过分析报告所举优秀案例的相似点和不同点，确定欧洲和中国在城市可持续发展方面的潜在合作领域与方式。这些所选优秀案例只是欧洲城市计划资助项目的代表，以及中国城市可持续发展状况的一种写照。

　　欧洲和中国城市可持续发展的相似之处主要取决于双方共同面临的城市问题，而彼此的差异是由不同的城市化水平、社会经济发展阶段以及不同的治理和城市可持续发展模式造成的。我们可从调查案例中发现以下两大差异。

　　第一，规模和发展方式不同。总的来说，欧洲是从项目入手，它在城市层面实施了更多的城市可持续发展项目，重点是测试框架、方法和创新技术，推广已被测试和得到认可的示范项目。中国则在城市层面做了更多努力，更加重视试点城市可持续发展项目的实施，以及选择更多符合条件的城市来参与和开展相关项目。

第二，公共参与情况不同。欧洲和中国的公共参与方式并不相同。根据报告所举案例，欧洲项目与中国城市的项目相比更为重视公共参与和共同创造。这可能是由于双方的治理方法存在差异：中国城市的方法多为自上而下，而欧洲城市采用了自上而下与自下而上的混合模式。

除了规模、政策与治理方法不同之外，这些案例很好证明了城市转型需要采取综合措施，需要各类行动者和利益攸关方共同参与。一般而言，城市可持续发展存在以下三个主要推动因素：（1）拥有有助于应对特定城市挑战的新技术解决方案或社会创新；（2）新的治理模式以及公共行政能力与专业知识能够充分利用这些新的技术和社会机会，并能为城市转型创建框架；（3）提高公民对新方法和解决方案的认识，尽早参与城市规划和地方发展，推动行为改变并为新方案的采用提供支持。

据此，所有层面和利益攸关方均需努力实现城市可持续发展，并通过研究和创新为其提供有力支持。为了应对这种复杂性，地方或城市层面的实验可通过当地试点项目或创新应用实验室来帮助解决特定挑战，促使所有利益攸关方进行合作、共创和参与城市发展行动。这么做可帮助良好做法留下痕迹，继而总结经验并广泛推广——其中包括新的政策、合作伙伴关系或商业模式。报告所举事例突出了这种多元化利益攸关方方法的潜力，并为欧洲和中国行动者进一步展开交流提供了有趣参考。

城市可持续发展是一个复杂而漫长的过程，因此任何一个利益攸关方都无法单独实现这一目标。它需要各个利益攸关方，比如城市、企业、大学、研究机构和金融机构共同合作。由于双方存在上述差异，因此应更好地了解当地知识和需求，探索彼此的市场。

总的来说，欧洲可与中国的主要利益攸关方合作，分享已经检测和得到认可的示范项目，为中国城市提供城市可持续发展框架和经验（在开放数据和城市创新应用实验室等相关领域）。

中国拥有巨大的市场和创新友好型环境，可与欧洲的主要利益攸关方合作，为欧洲城市提供信息和网络技术，进行物理基础设施建设。

要调动和整合双方主要利益攸关方的资源，还需要建立合作伙伴关系。

从欧洲城市计划和中国城市中心在欧洲和中国的行动与工作领域来看（如前文所述），这两个组织各自发挥的促进作用极具意义。我们建议的合作方式可能包括但不限于以下方面：

以欧洲和中国城市为示范或观察城市，开展由双方主要利益攸关方参与的合作项目；举办活动，收集欧洲和中国专家以及主要利益攸关方的专业知识，以更好地了解当地知识、交流可被地方借鉴和调整的观点和经验。

China-EU Sustainable Development Research Group

by

JPI Urban Europe (JPI UE) and
China Center for Urban Development (CCUD)

Authors:

Manfred HORVAT, JPI UE

Margit NOLL, JPI UE

Johannes RIEGLER, JPI UE

Magnus BRINK, JPI UE

Katarina SCHYLBERG, JPI UE

Chengcheng WU, CCUD

Yue LIU, CCUD

Peiqi ZHU, CCUD

Kui FENG, CCUD

Bo FENG, CCUD

Shaokun WEI, CCUD

Jinjing ZHANG, CCUD

Preface

For supporting urban transitions globally, partnerships with strong commitments and cooperation on all scales, from local to global are required. Bilateral and multilateral partnerships between organisations, cities, programmes and initiatives can enhance international support for effective and targeted capacity-building to support national plans. Exchange and co-creation of knowledge, technologies and experiences regarding sustainable city services and infrastructures offer promising prospects for addressing issues of urban planning, environment, health, water, transport, ICT, hazards, resilience and disaster risk reduction, and improving the well-being of citizens.

In this sense, JPI Urban Europe (JPI UE) and China Center for Urban Development (CCUD) cooperate and collaborate with a focus on exchanging knowledge, establishing a dialogue on strategic level and bundling expertise of European and Chinese experts since 2016.

JPI UE is a challenge-driven research and innovation initiative of 20 countries. Since 2012, the programme has funded 67 projects in the area of sustainable and liveable urban areas. CCUD is a specialised agency directly under the National Development and Reform Commission (NDRC). CCUD is a specialist agency dedicated in policy research and consulting service on urbanization and urban development, which is engaged in providing policy research and consulting services in urbanization for NDRC and other relevant departments, participating in major researches at department and local levels, offering integrated services for urbanization and carrying out international cooperation. Given the fields of action and work of JPI UE and CCUD, the established and successful partnership between both agencies contributes to localizing and implementing the Sustainable Development Goals and New Urban Agenda in Europe and in China by exchanging knowledge, stimulating discussions and underlining the importance.

Margit Noll, Chair of the
Management Board,
JPI Urban Europe

Shi Yulong, Director General,
Research Fellow, China Center
for Urban Development

April, 2019

Contents

Abstract

In recent years, the global perception of urban areas has changed. An urban area was often described as a place where societal challenges were manifested in space in terms of pollution, congestion, health risks, etc. It is now described as a place where the concentration of economic and social activity is perceived as an asset for transformative change. The rapid and unprecedented scale of urbanisation, despite challenges that it brought about, can mainly be understood as a process of opportunities to facilitate urban transitions.

1. SDGs: A Global Reference for Sustainable Urban Development

On a global scale, the transformative power of urbanisation for tackling global societal challenges has been recognised and expressed intensively in current global policies, agendas and guidelines. In *the* 2030 *Agenda for Sustainable Development*, the United Nations outlines 17 Sustainable Development Goals (SDGs) which "will stimulate action over the next 15 years in areas of critical importance for humanity and the planet"[1]. The importance of urban areas for achieving the SDGs becomes evident when looking at the roles they are assigned in the document—*the SDG* 11 *Sustainable Cities and Communities* is entirely dedicated to urbanisation but also the remaining 16 SDGs have an urban dimension. The 17 SDGs and their targets clearly underline the importance of sustainable urban development for the future of humanity and the planet, and 90 out of the 169 indicators encompass urban areas.

The SDG 11 expresses the need to discuss sustainable urbanisation and urban development in politics, policy and practice for the first time at global level. Connected to the SDG 11, UN-Habitat published *the New Urban Agenda* which was signed by almost all member states. *The New Urban Agenda* illustrates a shared vision of

---

①   United Nations, Transforming our World: The 2030 Agenda for Sustainable Development, 2015, p. 3.

urbanisation that can contribute to a sustainable future offering benefits and opportunities for all. It marks a paradigm shift identifying sustainable urban development as part of the solution to societal challenges. The SDG 11 and *the New Urban Agenda* provide a global reference framework for goals and visions of sustainable pathways with global consensus of importance.

The visions and pathways mentioned above represent a paradigm shift from understanding urbanization as an undesirable dynamic resulting in environmental and social challenges to a process with transformative power[1]. However, approaches towards such sustainable transformation are manifold and diverse, which include a broad range of initiatives, activities, programs, projects, methodologies and stakeholders. To realise the above-mentioned urban transitions, the multiplicity of approaches in urban policy as well as research and innovation require navigation across sectoral silos, approaches, and technologies[2]. At the same time awareness is needed on where and how they add up and increase the transformative

---

[1] Foreword by Joan Clos in: UN-Habitat, National Urban Policy: A Guiding Framework, 2015.

[2] Bylund, J. , Connecting the Dots by Obstacles? Friction and Traction Ahead for the SRIA Urban Transitions Pathway, 2016.

potential and where conflicting strategies, approaches and implementations cause dilemmas and might limit the transformative power.

2. Benefitting from International Exchange

For supporting urban transitions globally, partnerships with strong commitments and cooperation on all scales are required, from local to global. Bilateral and multilateral partnerships between organisations, cities, programmes and initiatives can enhance international support for effective and targeted capacity building. The exchange and co-creation of knowledge, technologies and experiences regarding sustainable city services and infrastructures offer promising prospects for addressing issues in urban planning, environment, health, water, transport, ICT, hazards, resilience and disaster risk reduction, and improving the well-being of citizens.

In this sense, JPI Urban Europe (hereinafter referred to as the "JPI UE") and the China Center for Urban Development (hereinafter referred to as the "CCUD") have collaborated since 2016, with a focus on exchanging knowledge, establishing a dialogue on strategic level and bundling expertise of European and Chinese experts.

JPI UE is a European challenge-driven research and innovation initiative. Since 2012, it has funded more than 70 projects in the area of sustainable and liveable urban areas with strong emphasis on Urban Living Labs, experimentation and science-policy cooperation. CCUD is a public institution under the National Development and Reform Commission (NDRC). CCUD is specialized in policy research and consultancy on urbanization and urban development. Since its establishment in 1998, it has been conducting policy research and providing consulting services at ministerial and local levels and offering integrated services for urbanization and carrying out international cooperation. Given the fields of action and work of JPI UE and CCUD, the established and successful partnership between the two organisations contributes to localizing and implementing the SDGs and *the New Urban Agenda* in Europe and China by exchanging knowledge, stimulating discussions and raising awareness of good practices concerning urban transitions.

3. Innovative Approaches and Case Studies from Europe and China

Five thematic areas of sustainable urban development have

been selected to present European and Chinese cases. For each thematic area, a research and innovation project funded by JPI UE and innovative projects in Chinese cities are used as cases to underline good practices and highlight innovative approaches conducive to achieving SDGs. The following are overviews of the good practices by thematic area in this report.

1. 1. Sustainable Urban Planning and Urban Renewal

People centred urban planning and the renewal of the existing housing stock towards energy efficiency and for enhancing the quality of life of the residents are key to sustainable urban development. To this end, the example of the project SubUrbanLab shows cases how co-design in urban living labs and participatory planning can modernize and socially uplift underprivileged neighbourhoods. In Chinese cities, the development of superblocks has hindered the walkability in urban areas and contributed to urban sprawl. The large-scale renewal project in Nanchong Prefecture (Sichuan Province) illustrates how urban planning and renewal can contribute to the human scale developments by promoting a multi-centric urban structure and thus enhance walkability, access to public parks and thus contribute to sustainable and liveable urban areas.

1. 2. **Energy Efficiency and Low-carbon Development**

Urban areas have great potential to reduce greenhouse gas e-missions and increase energy efficiency, thus contributing to actions of climate change mitigation. This does not only require renewable energy technologies or innovative energy management but also changing user behaviours. In this sense, the project me[2] aims at creating a community platform to increase awareness of the energy consumption among citizens and investigate ways to change user behaviours towards greater energy efficiency. The me[2] concept was tested in two Urban Living Labs in Amsterdam (the Netherlands) and Lisbon (Portugal). In China, efforts have been made at the strategic level and/or on the city scale. Several Chinese ministries have promoted sustainable urban development by launching eco-cities policies, standards and pilot programmes for low carbon development. A large number of cities in China have made efforts to achieve low carbon development. One of the best cases in China, Hangzhou City, followed an ambitious plan to become a low-carbon city and a role model for sustainable development in the country.

1. 3. **Transport and Mobility**

Efforts are made worldwide to improve mobility systems with the aim to provide safe access for all people to public places, goods, services and economic opportunities, while at the same time reducing the environmental footprint of transportation. Tackling the transport and mobility issue has a significant impact on other (socio-) economic and environmental aspects as well as on the quality of life and the wellbeing of the urban populations. For this thematic area, multi-modal mobility systems and new mobility services were investigated to deal with problems of commuting and congestion. The European case study, the JPI UE project Smart Commuting analysed mobility behaviours of commuters in three countries to identify the need for and potential of new mobility services. Results of this project have not only been reflected in policies but are also translated into business solutions with transportation companies. The case of Shanghai in China illustrates how different smart services can enhance the multimodal transport behaviour where busses, cars, trains and bikes play an essential role. Through an innovative app solution, different transport modes are connected, and door-to-door travel planning is offered in a multi-modal way.

1. 4. Sharing Economy

With the development of digital technologies, the sharing economy has become a reality. Combined with an upcoming tendency among urban populations towards sharing instead of owning, sharing services are influencing urban life socially, environmentally and e-conomically. Sharing economy provides potential to challenge established routines. In Europe and China, new sharing schemes are significantly influencing urban life, consumption patterns and have the potential to significantly contribute to sustainable urban development. The JPI UE project E4 – share developed models for flexible, efficient and economic viable electric car-sharing systems. In the project, different car-sharing models were compared, user incentives determined, and supporting policy frameworks investigated using the case of the City of Vienna. In China, the sharing economy has seen significant growth recently. As part of sharing economy, the Public Bicycle program was first launched in Hangzhou in 2008 as a seamless feeder service to public transit throughout the city in light of growing traffic congestion and environmental concerns. With the development of innovative technologies, the dock-less bike sharing in China has seen a rapid expansion since 2015. New sharing schemes and business models have created a boom of Bike Sharing in China ever since. Today, bike sharing is especially relevant for solving the issue of "the last mile", the distance between public transportation and people's final destination and contributes to the reduction of car dependency and greenhouse gas emissions.

1. 5. **Smart Urban Governance**

To effectively implement and design strategies for sustainable urban development, new collaborative governance processes involving private and public stakeholders are called for. Enabling technologies, big data and "real time" action offer new ways for innovative and smart urban governance and management. Multiple information sources are nowadays easily available for urban decision making, while appropriate tools and methods are required to consolidate and synthesise them. The JPI UE project UrbanData2Decide processed information from public social media and open data libraries to develop a decision support system for urban governance. At the same time digital technologies and social media support participatory planning and governance. Another JPI UE project Incubators for Public Space embedded such new technologies in participatory planning processes to allow all stakeholders to contribute to urban planning. The project implemented Urban Living Labs in London, Brussels and Turin. In China, progress and institutional breakthroughs have been made in smart urban governance in the past few years, with the application of more advanced information and network technology. "Internet + " has transformed urban management model and service provision and delivery models in a profound way.

Smarter ways to manage population and monitor urban road networks and the smart emergency response system are among the typical examples of smart urban governance. So far, 80 cities have carried out the "Information-for-the Public" pilot projects. The e-governance has increased government efficiency. The online service platforms introduced in Shandong, Zhejiang and Guangdong provinces have helped innovate and improve government services, transparency and law enforcement supervision. The Smart Urban Governance approach of Weihai City (Shandong Province) aimed at tapping the potential of smart technologies by fostering institutional change, capacity building in public administration and socio-technological innovations.

4. Conclusions

The Conclusions section is intended to identify potential areas and ways of collaboration between Europe and China in sustainable urban development by analysing similarities and differences based on the good practices that are presented in this report. The good practices are selective rather than exhaustive, which represent, to some extent, related projects that have been funded by JPI UE and represent the sustainable urban development landscape in China.

The similarities in sustainable urban development between Europe and China are largely due to common urban challenges that both sides are facing. The differences are caused by different levels of urbanization, stages of socio-economic development as well as different approaches to governance and sustainable urban development between the two sides in general. The following two main differences can be determined from the cases investigated.

- *Different Scales and Ways to Scale up.* In general, the European side has implemented more sustainable urban development projects in European cities on the project scale, which focuses on testing frameworks, approaches and / or innovative technologies and on the rollout of the already tested and approved demonstration projects. While the Chinese side has made more efforts on the city scale, which puts more emphasis on implementing projects concerning sustainable urban development in pilot cities and selecting and involving more eligible cities to start related projects.

- *Different Ways to Engage the Public.* Different ways have been witnessed on both sides in pubic engagement. According to the cases reflected in the report participatory approaches and co-creation methods are more strongly applied in European projects than the projects in Chinese cities. This may be due to the different governance approaches, a more top-down approach in Chinese cities, compared to a mixed model of top-down and bottom-up approaches in European cities.

Besides those differences in scale, policy and governance approaches, the cases very well demonstrate that urban transitions requires integrated approaches and the involvement of different actors and stakeholders. In principle the following three main elements are key for driving sustainable urban development.

• Availability of new technological solutions or social innovations that help to tackle a specific urban challenge;

• New governance models as well as capacities and expertise in public administration fit to take highest advantage of such new technological and social opportunities and to create frameworks for urban transitions;

• Mobilisation of citizens to create awareness of new approaches and solutions, drive behaviour change and support uptake of new solutions through early involvement in urban planning and local development.

According to this, efforts are needed on all scales and of all stakeholder groups to achieve sustainable urban development and research and innovation can strongly support these. To deal with this complexity, experimental settings on local or city level can help addressing specific challenges, through local pilot projects or living labs, allowing all stakeholders to cooperate, co-create, engage in urban development actions. Through this evidence can be created for good practice and conclusions can be drawn for wider implementation, including new policies, partnerships or business models. The examples given in the report highlight the potential of such multi-stakeholder approaches and create interesting references for further exchange between European and Chinese actors.

As sustainable urban development is a complex, long-term process, no single stakeholder can achieve the goal alone. Rather, it requires the collaboration among various stakeholders, such as cities, businesses, universities/research institutes and financial institutions. As the two sides are different in the above-mentioned aspects, it could be worth exploring each other's market by better understanding local knowledge and needs. In general, the Europe side could provide Chinese cities with sustainable urban development framework and experiences (in related areas such as open data and urban living labs) by sharing its already tested and approved demonstration projects in collaboration with Chinese key stakeholders.

China has a huge market with enabling environment for innovation and could provide information and network technologies and physical infrastructure construction in European cities where needed in collaboration with European key stakeholders. Partnerships may be needed to mobilize and integrate resources from the key stakeholders on both sides. Given the fields of action and work of JPI UE and CCUD in Europe and China mentioned earlier, it could be helpful for the two organisations to play a facilitator role on each side. Suggested ways of cooperation may include, but not limited to the following: conducting cooperative projects involving key stakeholders from both sides, with European and Chinese cities as demonstrator and/or observer cities; and organising events to gather expertise of European and Chinese experts and key stakeholders to better understand local knowledge as well as exchange ideas and experiences that could be transferable and adapt to other local contexts.

Chapter One

Introduction

1. Background

In recent years, the global perception of the urban area has changed. An urban area was often described as a place where societal challenges were manifested in space in terms of pollution, congestion, health risks, etc. , while it is now described as a place where the concentration of socio-economic activities is perceived as an asset for transformational change.

Among others, urbanisation is an important driver for such transformational change. In 2014, 54% of the world population lived in urban areas; the figure is estimated to be about 67% in

2050[1]. According to projections by the United Nations the global urban population will increase from 3.6 billion in 2011 to 5.3 billion in 2050[2]. That is the most substantial change of human settlement in history.

There are differences in urbanization processes and patterns as well as the level of urbanization between the developed and the developing world[3]. In the developed world, a balancing process can be observed with the population decreasing in large cities and increasing in smaller or medium-sized cities. The situation in developing countries is rather characterised by large cities attracting more people and maximizing the positive externalities and minimizing the negative impacts"[4], which imposes a challenge for

---

[1] World Urbanisation Prospects—United Nations Department of Economic and Social Affairs, Population Division, 2014; J. Clos, " A 21st Century Vision for Urbanisation", OECD Development Matters, 8 June 2016.

[2] O. Courtard, G. Finnveden, S. Kabitsch, R. Kitchin, R. Matos, P. Nijkamp, C. Pronello, D. Robinson, Urban Megatrends: Towards a European Research Agenda; A Report by the Scientific Advisory Board of the Joint Programming Initiative Urban Europe, 2014, p. 3; World Urbanisation Prospects—United Nations Department of Economic and Social Affairs, Population Division, 2014.

[3] Urban Europe—Statistics on Cities, Towns and Suburbs, Statistical Books, Eurostat, 2016, p. 8.

[4] UN-Habitat, The Economic Role of Cities, United Nations Settlements Programme, Nairobi, 2011, p. 41.

national governments and municipal authorities. In developing countries, urbanization is an ongoing important phenomenon and it is expected that more than 90% of future urban growth will happen in developing countries[1]. Developing countries are expected to accommodate over 80% of the world urban population by 2050 since rural-urban migrants seek a better life for themselves and their families in urban areas[2].

Substantial differences also have been observed by continent, region and country. Such differences can be seen from Figure 1 and 2. In Europe and North America, urbanization has been closely linked with industrialization in the 19th century and the first half of the 20th century[3]. The process slowed down after that because suburbanisation leads to the reduction in population in urban areas.

---

① Q. Z. Zhang, "The Trends, Promises and Challenges of Urbanisation in the World", *Habitat International*, 54, 2016, pp. 241 – 254; O. Courtard, G. Finnveden, S. Kabitsch, R. Kitchin, R. Matos, P. Nijkamp, C. Pronello, D. Robinson, Urban Megatrends: Towards a European Research Agenda; A Report by the Scientific Advisory Board of the Joint Programming Initiative Urban Europe, 2014, p. 3.

② O. Courtard, G. Finnveden, S. Kabitsch, R. Kitchin, R. Matos, P. Nijkamp, C. Pronello, D. Robinson, Urban Megatrends: Towards a European Research Agenda; A Report by the Scientific Advisory Board of the Joint Programming Initiative Urban Europe, 2014, p. 3.

③ Q. Z. Zhang, "The Trends, Promises and Challenges of Urbanisation in the World", *Habitat International*, 54, 2016, pp. 241 – 252.

There are different reasons or drivers for suburbanisation, such as lower costs of housing, increasing private car ownership, better connections between the center and the periphery due to the development of the public transport, green and more pleasant and liveable environment, clean air, tranquillity, closeness to nature, alternative employment opportunities, better level of safety compared to city centers, and demographic change.

According to most recent data[1], there are currently 31 cities with the population of 10 million or more in the world—17 in Asia, 5 in Latin America, 4 in Europe, 3 in Africa, and 2 in North America. There are 6 cities with the population of more than 10 million in China, 5 in India, 2 in Brazil and Japan, and 16 in other countries. By 2030, it is expected that the number of mega-cities with 10 million or more inhabitants will increase to 41 in the world[2]. Such rapid and unprecedented scale of urbanisation and the concentration of population in large or mega-cities in the world have caused continuous challenges but meanwhile provide

---

[1] World City Population 2018, see: http://worldpopulationreview.com/world-cities.

[2] World Urbanisation Prospects, United Nations Department of Economic and Social Affairs, Population Division, 2014, p. 1.

opportunities to facilitate such urban transformation.

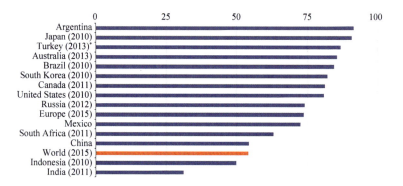

Figure 1　Share of urban population, 2014

（ % of total population living in cities）

Notes：① United Nations data are based on national definitions; as such there may be a discrepancy with respect to the Eurostat data used elsewhere in this publication. ② * Estimate.

Source：Urban Europe—Statistics on Cities, Towns and Suburbs, 2016, p. 8.

For instance, the large number of rural-urban migrants in the process of rapid urbanization leads to growth of urban agglomerations. This causes substantial challenges in urban areas and meanwhile offers competitive advantages and opportunities for a better life. The relationship between urbanization and socio-economic development in urban areas is complex. Thus, many preconditions for urban development, such as job opportunities, infrastructure, public services as well as possible impacts regarding CO_2 emissions, climate change, water resources, biodiversity, social inclusion and human health, need to be re-assessed in order to enforce positive aspects of sustainable urbanization[1].

There is no commonly agreed-upon definition of sustainable urbanization. However, it is useful to reflect on related definitions in order to see the spectrum of perspectives that are necessary to comprehend the holistic nature of sustainable urban development. Sustainable urbanization requires multidisciplinary approaches addressing water, air, soil, energy, food, transportation, land, biodiversity, chemicals, construction, climate change (both adaptation and mitigation) economic development and social change in integrative and interactive ways rather than by "silo thinking" in separated disciplines[2].

---

[1] UN-Habitat, The Economic Role of Cities. United Nations Human Settlements Programme, Nairobi, 2011; M. Chen, H. Zhang, W. Liu, W. Zhang, "The Global Pattern of Urbanization and Economic growth: Evidence from the Last Three Decades", *PLOS ONE*, 2014, 9, 8, p. 14.

[2] Sustainable Urbanization Policy Brief. Proliferation of Urban Centres, their Impact on the World's environment and the Potential Role of Global Environment Facility (GERF), Scientific and Technical Advisory Panel, 2014, p. 4.

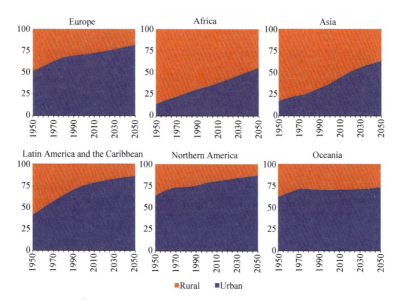

Figure 2   The Estimated and Projected Urban and Rural

Populations in the World from 1950 to 2050

Notes: United Nations data are based on national definitions; as such there may be a discrepancy with respect to the Eurostat data used elsewhere in this publication.

Source: World Urbanization Prospects—United Nations, Department of Economic and Social Affairs, Publication Division, 2014.

This report adopts the following definition given by ICLEI Local Governments for Sustainability 2016: "Sustainable cities work towards an environmentally, socially, and economically healthy and resilient habitat for existing populations, without compromising the ability of future generations to experience the same. " ①

2. Global Trends, Opportunities and Challenges of Sustainable Urban Development

JPI Urban Europe's Scientific Advisory Board in its 2014 report② identified a number of global trends.

International trade, the creation of multinational companies, increased export-orientation, the development institutions like the World Trade organisation (WTO) and agreements that make trade and investment easier, are elements of the globalised economy. Developments in information and communication technologies as well as in the transport sector supported a steep increase in global interaction and cooperation. Economic relations are bound into different kinds of global chains of connectedness. Economic globalisation was and is a key driver of urbanization and cities and city clusters are focal sites for production and consumption attracting

---

① http: //www. iclei. org/activities/agendas/sustainable-city. html.

② O. Courtard, G. Finnveden, S. Kabitsch, R. Kitchin, R. Matos, P. Nijkamp, C. Pronello, D. Robinson, Urban Megatrends: Towards a European Research Agenda: A Report by the Scientific Advisory Board of the Joint Programming Initiative Urban Europe, 2014.

people at all levels of competences, capabilities and skills, acting as local-global nodes of interconnection.

At the same time, modernization of agriculture leads to decreasing job opportunities on the country side and is another driver causing people moving to cities.

Geopolitics and conflict influence urbanization and urban development. Since the Second World War, with the formation of the United Nations and other intergovernmental bodies, a complex system of multi-level consultation, management, and governance has been established that influences also urban governance and management. Although, international bodies were founded in order to support peace, conflicts are still the reason for transnational migration. In addition, climate change causes people to leave their region or country where they do not find adequate living conditions anymore.

At international level, emerging countries (E7: China, India, Brazil, Mexico, Russia, Indonesia, and Turkey) gained political power and influence on the global stage and a multi-polar global political system has developed. At local level, in many countries cities achieved more and more autonomy and urban governance and management plays an important role with city mayors as key agents of change.

"Demographic change results from a combination of migration, both rural-urban and cross-border, as well as due to gradual changes in life-expectancy and birth rate. "[1] The global population is increasing and for 2050 is expected to peak at 9. 3 billion with growth concentrating mainly in developing countries.

Improved living conditions will lead to decreasing mortality rates and ageing of the population. These developments will have important consequences for the labour market, housing, services, consumption patterns and adequate provisions of care for the elderly.

As " cities are agents of social, cultural, economic, technological and political changes and advancement", there are many possible positive effects and opportunities of urbanization, such as[2]: economic development and employment opportunities, developments of new markets, gains of higher productivity,

---

[1]   O. Courtard, G. Finnveden, S. Kabitsch, R. Kitchin, R. Matos, P. Nijkamp, C. Pronello, D. Robinson, Urban Megatrends: Towards a European Research Agenda: A Report by the Scientific Advisory Board of the Joint Programming Initiative Urban Europe, 2014, p. 5.

[2]   Q. Z. Zhang, "The trends, Promises and Challenges of Urbanisation in the World", *Habitat International*, 54, 2016.

benefitting from proximity and low transport costs, cities as centers offering different services, education and health care, innovation, culture and creativity, as well as local-global linkages.

The opportunities and challenges of urbanisation and urban development need to be addressed by policies, plans, and programmes of action designed for specific situations following the requirements of sustainable development as defined and agreed upon on international level.

Although cities across all continents face in principle the same challenges, the pathways towards sustainable urban development need to correspond to the cities' specific urban situation, anticipate its cultural, infrastructure, economic, social characteristics and dynamics. In addition, size matters and there are significant differences between megacities and small and medium sized towns. On the other side, the challenges that cities are facing put cities in a position to become vanguards of change towards sustainability and cities " are emerging as privileged grounds for effective environmental action" [1].

---

[1] UN-Habitat, *Urbanization and Development: Emerging Future*. Key Findings and Messages, *World Cities Report 2016*, United Nations Human Settlements Programme (UN-Habitat), 2016, p. 18.

In general, in the frame of adequate national strategies that follow global agreements and goals, urban leadership and authorities need to develop new strategies and apply new management approaches fit to cope with the complexities of the problems and creating new opportunities.

Urbanization created substantial environmental challenges due to industrial activities, transportation, construction activities, heating, increasing energy demands, different kinds of waste, sanitation, pollution of air, water and soil, land use and urban sprawl, and lack or degradation of green areas.

There is wide spectrum of challenges and problems that may arise and that need to be considered in systematic planning and managing urban development as far as possible, such as[1]: (1) Urban sprawl, problems of land management, land use, urban agriculture, degradation of land and ecosystems; (2) Center-periphery differences, commuting time, unequal distribution of services; (3) Lack of adequate investment in housing leading to shortages of affordable housing and formation of slums; (4) Higher

---

[1]　See: Q. Z. Zhang, "The Trends, Promises and Challenges of Urbanisation in the World", *Habitat International*, 54, 2016.

costs of living, risks of unemployment, risk of poverty and social exclusion; (5) Urban inequalities and gender inequality, disparity between rich and poor, social segregation, inequalities hitting girls and women more severely than boys and women; (6) Shortage of infrastructure investment, deficits regarding safe water supply, problems of waste management and treatment (private and industrial), sewage treatment, lack of adequate sanitation services; (7) Traffic congestions and emissions from cars, industry, and heating with coal; (8) Environmental degradation, especially contamination of water, air, and soils, noise light stress, greenhouse gas emissions, problems of waste management and treatment; (9) Crime and insecurity, areas becoming ungovernable, increase of gated communities and operations of private security operators leading to segregation and increased distrust between different societal communities and groupings.

It is necessary to emphasize that these challenges are interdependent and need to be addressed taking systems-oriented approaches.

Cities may lack sufficient resources for fulfilling the necessary tasks and coping with the multitude of challenges. In developing countries, urbanization is an ongoing important phenomenon and it is expected that future urban growth will happen to more than 90% in developing countries[1]. However, also there will be substantial differences between regions and countries. In the developed world, a balancing process can be observed with the population decreasing in large cities and increasing in smaller or medium-sized cities. The situation in developing countries is rather characterised by large cities attracting more people and maximizing the positive externalities and minimizing the negative impacts"[2] is a challenge for national governments and municipal authorities.

3. The Global Framework for Sustainable Urban Development and Latest Achievements

On a global scale, the transformative power of urbanisation for tackling global societal challenges has been recognised and expressed intensively in recent global policies, agendas and guidelines. The United Nations, in its 2030 Agenda for Sustainable

---

[1] Q. Z. Zhang, "The Trends, Promises and Challenges of Urbanisation in the World", *Habitat International*, 54, 2016.

[2] UN-Habitat, *Urbanization and Development: Emerging Future*. Key Findings and Messages, *World Cities Report 2016*, United Nations Human Settlements Programme (UN-Habitat), 2016, p. 41.

Development, formulated 17 Sustainable Development Goals (SDGs) which "*will stimulate action over the next* 15 *years in areas of critical importance for humanity and the planet*"[①]. The importance of urban areas for achieving the SDGs becomes evident when looking at the prominent roles they are given in the document: SDG 11 is entirely dedicated to Sustainable Cities and Communities, while all 17 SDGs have an urban dimension. Furthermore, 90 out of the 169 indicators encompass urban areas. The 17 SDGs and its targets clearly underline the importance of sustainable urbanisation for the future of humanity and the planet.

SDG 11 expresses the need to discuss sustainable urbanisation and urban development in politics, policy and practice for the first time on global level. Connected to the SDG 11, UN-Habitat published the New Urban Agenda which was signed by almost all member states. The New Urban Agenda illustrates a shared vision of urbanisation that can contribute to a sustainable future offering benefits and opportunities for all. Foremost the New Urban Agenda marks a paradigm shift identifying sustainable urban development as

---

① United Nations, Transforming our world: The 2030 Agenda for Sustainable Development, 2015, https://sustainabledevelopment.un.org/post2015/transformingourworld, p. 3.

part of the solution to societal challenges. SDG 11 and the New Urban Agenda are providing a global reference framework for goals and visions for sustainable pathways with significant global consensus[1].

（In SDG 11 and the New Urban Agenda）It is acknowledged that cities are drivers of progress and not solely a source of problems and risks, which can be seen as paradigm shift. Urban development is crucial for reaching the sustainable development goals, because more than half of the global population is living in urban areas nowadays and this number continues to grow[2].

The visions and pathways expressed in SDG 11 and the *New Urban Agenda* are related to the paradigm shift in understanding urbanization rather as a process with transformative power[3] than an

---

① JPI Urban Europe Scientific Advisory Board, New Urban Transitions towards Sustainability. Manuscript in preparation, 2018.

② Ibid. .

③ Foreword by Joan Clos in: UN-Habitat, National Urban Policy: A Guiding Framework, 2015, https: //unhabitat. org/books/national-urban-policy-a-guiding-framework/.

undesirable dynamic resulting in environmental and social challenges and problems. However, approaches towards sustainable transformation are manifold, diverse and include a broad range of activities, methodologies, programs, projects, stakeholders and initiatives. This multiplicity of approaches in urban policy as well as research and innovation call for urban transitions[1] that navigate between sectoral silos, approaches, technologies[2], and analyse where they add up and increase the transformative potential. At the same time, conflicting targets and strategies need to be identified as they might hinder the transformative power and therewith, limit urban transitions.

There are different possible approaches towards pursuing sustainable urban development by focussing on specific targets as appropriate to the specific situation of a particular urban area. In

---

[1]   Urban Transitions are defined as "fundamental and multi-dimensional alterations of urban development to reach the ambitious targets concerning ensuring livelihoods of citizens by avoiding greater stress on environment and fair distribution of economic and natural resources"; in JPI UE (2015) SRIA Strategic Research and Innovation Agenda. See: https://jpi-urbaneurope.eu/documents_ library/.

[2]   Bylund, J., Connecting the Dots by Obstacles? Friction and Traction Ahead for the SRIA Urban Transitions Pathway, Joint Programming Initiative Urban Europe, 2016.

the same year of the publication of the SDGs, Hassan and Lee[1] investigated in an in-depth literature study issues that were identified as highly relevant to sustainable urban development in scientific papers published world-wide over five years, grouped as: (1) Balanced approach to SUD and socio-cultural awareness; (2)Economic sustainability and mitigating GHG; (3) City structure, land use, urban sprawl and sustainable transportation; (4) Economic urban development; (5) Urban renewal, urban vegetation and sustainable assessment systems; and (6) Assessing urban sustainability and applying urban experiments to different locations.

The study underlines that transportation and fostering educational awareness are top concerns in both quantitative and qualitative terms in the reviewed publications. Researchers agree that transportation policies can make important contributions to creating urban sustainability by measures such as promoting electrical cars or imposing tolls on specific areas and investing in expanding public transport networks. There is not enough research

---

[1]   A. M. Hassan & H. Lee, "Toward the Sustainable Development of Urban Areas: An Overview of Global Trends in Trials and Policies", *Land us Policy*, 48, 2015.

on the connections between home and work and the possibilities of residents optimizing their living space in relation to commuting and job.

The study concludes that Europe was first in promoting sustainable urban development and reached an acceptable level of sustainable urban development before Asia. In Asian countries sustainable urban development is high on the agenda now, and China ranks first with regard to attention paid to sustainable urban development, while India ranks second.

In Europe, quantitative and qualitative issues center on restoring historic buildings, e. g. by improving their energy efficiency. Social participation and educational awareness are deemed important in scientific publications. In Asia, the following issues are most important in the scientific literature in quantitative terms: Land use, assessment of sustainability, urban sprawl, transportation, educational awareness, development of urban vegetation, and the need for establishing a balanced approach linking economic, social and ecological issues in a comprehensive way. In qualitative terms, the most relevant issues are educational awareness, social participation and urban land use. Out of USA, Latin America and Australia, awareness regarding sustainable urban development is highest in USA. USA, and also Canada and Australia try to reduce greenhouse gas emissions by lowering the number of cars. In USA, urban agriculture is on the agenda as a measure contributing towards achieving the goal of self-sufficient cities. In Africa, there are only few research activities regarding sustainable urban development due to the poor economic and political conditions of most African countries.

It is interesting to note that in the results of the analysis of scientific literature many important aspects are missing such as buildings, socio-economic aspects as well as the role of governance—to name just a few.

About three years after the SDGs were agreed upon, the UN reports about the state of play of the implementation of SDG 11 are as follows[1].

SDG 11: Make cities and human settlements inclusive, safe, resilient and sustainable

The pace of urban growth has been unprecedented. More

---

[1]   United Nations, *The Sustainable Development Goals Report 2017*, New York, 2017, p. 8.

than half the world's population, or nearly 4 billion people, lived in cities in 2015. However, while cities are incubators of innovation and help foster increased employment and economic growth, rapid urbanization has brought with it enormous challenges, including inadequate housing, increased air pollution, and lack of access to basic services and infrastructure.

The proportion of the urban population living in slums worldwide fell from 28 percent in 2000 to 23 percent in 2014. However, in sub-Saharan Africa, more than half (56 percent) of urban dwellers lived in slum conditions.

From 2000 to 2015, in all regions of the world, the expansion of urban land outpaced the growth of urban populations, resulting in urban sprawl.

According to data from cities in 101 countries from 2009 to 2013, approximately 65 percent of the population was served by municipal waste collection.

In 2014, 9 in 10 people living in urban areas breathed air that did not meet the World Health Organization's air quality guidelines value for particulate matter (PM 2. 5).

As of May 2017, 149 countries had fully or partially

implemented national-level urban policies, most of which are aligned with priority areas identified in the SDGs.

4. Aim of the Report

The report aims to provide an outlook for further needs and priorities concerning sustainable urban development in Europe and China by analysing main challenges and illustrating selected good practices from cities on both sides.

5. Structure of the Report

The report contains five chapters. Chapter One sets the scene for the research by putting sustainable urban development in the context of urbanization, SDGs and the New Urban Agenda. Chapter Two illustrates global trends, main challenges and key achievements in relation to sustainable urban development. Chapter Three analyses main challenges and strategies/approaches concerning sustainable urban development in Europe and China. Chapter Four presents selected good practices from cities on both sides, with a special focus on five themes. Chapter Five concludes the report by summarizing existing cooperative projects on sustainable urban development between both sides and providing an outlook for further needs and priorities.

Chapter Two

Main Challenges and Strategies/ Approaches Concerning Sustainable Urban Development in Europe and China

1. Main Challenges and Strategies/ Approaches in Europe

1. 1. The European Policy and Programme Context

The pattern of urbanisation in Europe differs significantly from other parts of the world. Europe is highly urbanised with around 73% of the population living in urban areas. The distinct characteristic of urbanisation in Europe is that in contrast to Asia and South and North America, Europe has a high number of small and medium sized cities and relatively few urban areas above 1 M inhabitants[1]. Only four out of 79 cities world-wide with a population over 5M are located in Europe. 16% of the European population live in cities with over 5M people compared to 30% in Asia and 28% in North America[2].

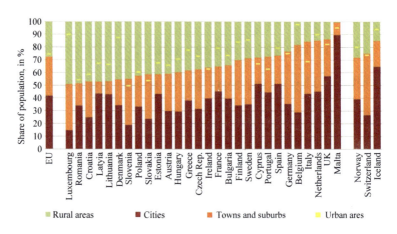

Figure 3　Population by Degree of Urbanisation per
EU Country in 2014

Source: European Commission and UN-Habitat: The State of the European Cities, 2016; Eurostat and World Urbanization Propstects, 2014.

---

① JPI Urban Europe, Strategic Research and Innovation Agenda, 2015, https: //jpi-urbaneurope. eu/documents_ library/.

② European Commission and UN-HABITAT, The State of the European Cities, 2016, http: //ec. europa. eu/regional _ policy/en/policy/themes/urban-development/ cities-report/.

Europe's urban areas are diverse in their forms, organisation, spatial dynamic, socio-economic structure and governance system. These different characteristics are historically grown, determined by trajectories and political form of organisation at a national and local level and resulted in contrasting forms of urban developments in south-eastern and north-western European countries. However, continental and global influences will *"ultimately need to be integrated in complex local conditions and requirements so that responses (strategies to bring about performance improvements) fit to their contexts"*[①].

The performance of European Cities[②] combined with the new policy framework of the 2030 Sustainable Development Goals have led to priority areas which are seen as key for the further development of European Urban Areas. These themes haven been taken up by the work of the Urban Agenda for the EU. The Urban Agenda for the EU (Pact of Amsterdam) is a coordinated and integrated approach to deal with the urban dimension of the EU and national policies and legislation. Therefore, 12 thematic

---

① JPI Urban Europe, Strategic Research and Innovation Agenda, 2015.
② As described extensively in: European Commission and UN-HABITAT, The State of the European Cities, 2016.

partnerships have been implemented where public authority, Member States, the European Commission and stakeholders such as NGOs or businesses are involved. The themes of the partnerships are among others Smart Land Use, Climate Adaptation, Circular Economy, Inclusion of Migrants and Refugees, Urban Mobility, Housing, Air Quality, Urban Poverty, Jobs and Skills in the Local Economy, Digital Transition and Public Procurement. The Urban Agenda for the EU is one commitment by the European Commission to localize and implement UN-Habitat's New Urban Agenda.

Important approaches, thematic areas and challenges in which big efforts are being made in Europe are among other smart cities and communities, climate change and the integration of refugees and migrants. Smart Cities and Communities refer to urban areas which make increasing use of ICT and in which (social) innovation plays a significant role. In this concept, ICT can be a main enabler for tackling societal challenges and to enhance the participation of society in urban development processed. Technological approaches which take particular respect to and include social processes, in short the link between innovation and society, make Smart Cities and Communities an important concept for urbanisation. Furthermore, in European cities great efforts for reducing greenhouse gas emissions, including increasing the energy efficiency of the existing building stock, have been made. Strategies and approaches to mitigate climate change are a common feature. In terms of adaptation to climate change, nature-based solution such as natural wetland, networks of green areas and greening of neighbourhoods and buildings have recently gained much attention[1]. Since the summer of 2015, in which many European countries and in particular urban areas were the destinations of big numbers of refugees, the integration and active involvement of the newly arrived gained in importance. The integration includes efforts and requires innovation in the education system, the housing sector and the labour market.

Besides the initiatives funded and supported by the European Commission and its Member States there are a number of relevant players and networks for sustainable urbanisation in Europe: ICLEI[2] (Local Governments for Sustainability); EUROCITIES[3] (a network of elected local and municipal governments of major European cities); ERRIN[4] (European Regions Research and

---

[1]　European Commission and UN-HABITAT, The State of the European Cities, 2016.

[2]　http://iclei-europe.org/home/.

[3]　http://www.eurocities.eu/.

[4]　https://www.errin.eu/.

Innovation Network), CEMR① (Council of European Municipalities and Regions) and UN-Habitat Europe②.

1. 2. **JPI Urban Europe: A Research and Innovation Programme Supporting Urban Transitions**

Urban development has gained increased attention in Europe over the recent years. Urban areas are hubs for regional—even national and continental—development and innovation. Providing harbours for refugees and migration and zones for climate change adaptation and sustainability, cities are key actors for addressing many of the societal challenges. As highlighted in the introduction already, urban areas play an essential role in achieving all of UN's 17 sustainable development goals in the 2030 *Agenda for Sustainable Development*, not merely goal number 11—*Sustainable Cities and Communities*.

JPI Urban Europe is thus committed to address the complexity of urban transitions by funding strategic research and innovation, improving and aligning R&I instruments, moderating science-policy processes and supporting transnational collaboration for local

---

① http://www.ccre.org/.
② https://unhabitat.org/tag/europe/.

capacity building. JPI Urban Europe connects public authorities, civil society, scientists, innovators, business and industry to provide an environment for urban research and innovation. The mission is to develop tools, knowledge and platforms for dialogue on urban transitions.

Complementary to the central concern of supporting transitions to urban sustainable and liveable futures, the JPI Urban Europe Strategic Research and Innovation Agenda published in 2015 sets out five thematic priorities to be tackled: Vibrancy in changing urban economies, Welfare and finance, Environmental sustainability and resilience, Accessibility and connectivity, Urban governance and participation.

For its implementation members from governments and funding organisations from 20 European countries are joining forces in several joint actions based on the portfolio of urban-related programmes and activities of each of the countries. In this sense the JPI Urban Europe functions as a platform for connecting and building upon these various programmes, benefitting from experiences and competences across borders. Our ambition is to provide an innovation eco system by engaging public and societal actors in the co-creation of missions and solutions, creating new

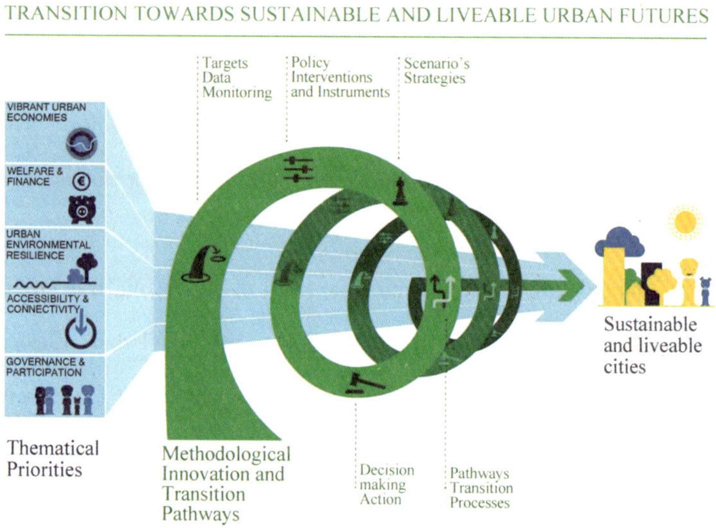

TRANSITION TOWARDS SUSTAINABLE AND LIVEABLE URBAN FUTURES

Figure 4　Framework of JPI Urban Europe's Strategic

Research and Innovation Agenda

kinds of partnerships to tackle the urban challenges.

2. Main Challenges and Strategies/ Approaches in China

China has witnessed accelerated urbanization of unprecedented scale in the past four decades since the country adopted the reform and opening-up policy in 1978. Its urbanization rate increased from only 18. 96% in 1979[1] to 51. 27% in 2010 and to 58. 52% in 2017, with the total urban population of 813. 47 million[2]. In the process, China has avoided some common negative impacts of rapid urbanization such as urban poverty and unemployment, with 260 million migrant workers[3] finding jobs in the secondary and tertiary industries in urban areas to contribute to its rapid economic growth, which, in turn, pulls 500 million people out of poverty in the country[4]. Urbanization in China has yet to be completed because the share of its urban population is still below expectations based on its current per capita income. China's urbanization rate is expected to be 65% in 2030 on current trends, with additional 20 million people living in urban areas each year[5].

---

[1]   UN-Habitat, *State of China's Cities 2010/2011: Better City, Better Life*, 2010, Foreign Languages Press.

[2]   National Bureau of Statistics of China.

[3]   The term *Migrant Worker* refers to people who were registered in rural areas or are holding rural *hukou* but living and working in urban areas. In general, migrant workers cannot have access to urban public services in the same way as residents who were registered in urban areas or are holding urban *hukou*.

[4]   World Bank and DRC, Urban China: Toward Efficient, Inclusive, and Sustainable Urbanization, 2014.

[5]   World Bank and DRC, Urban China: Toward Efficient, Inclusive, and Sustainable Urbanization, 2014; Wang, J. and He, D., " Sustainable Urban Development in China: Challenges and Achievements", *Mitigation and Adaptation Strategies for Global Change*, 20, 2015.

Such rural-urban migration of unprecedented scale in China is largely due to its rapid industrialization, with which its urban development pattern is featuring accelerated urban expansion and large energy consumption[1]. In the process of accelerated urbanization, cities are expanding significantly with rapid growing urban population, which has served as an important driver for economic growth and brought tremendous benefit to their stakeholders[2]. But meanwhile, the rapid pace of urban expansion and population growth have resulted in various challenges for sustainable urban development, such as urban sprawl, traffic congestion, excessive consumption of energy and environmental degradation[3].

These challenges are complex and intertwined largely because China's rapid economic growth has been driven by investment and

① Wei, H. , "The Strategy for China's Urban Transformation in the New Era", In: *China Economic Forum on Urban Transformation and Green Development*, 2014, Beijing: China Social Sciences Press.

② Tan, Y. , Xu, H. and Zhang, X. , "Sustainable Urbanization in China: A Comprehensive Literature Review", *Cities*, 55, 2016, pp. 82 – 93.

③ Qiu B. , On the New of the New Type of Urbanization, 2016, http: //kns. cnki. net/KCMS/detail/detail. aspx? dbcode = CFJD&dbname = CJFDTEMN&filename = ZFGP201600007&v = MjY1NTBoMVQzcVRyV00xRnJDVVJMS2ZaT1JyRnlIblVMelBQeX ZNZnJHNEg5Zk1yNDlGWTRSOGVYMUx1eFlTN0Q = .

its urbanization has relied excessively on land conversion and land financing over the past decades[1]. This, to some extent, is reflected in its typical urban development pattern over the last thirty years that is the single-use areas of urban blocks at large scales[2]. Many traditional residential communities in city centers have been demolished, resulting in their residents being relocated to suburban areas where suburban clusters or new towns have been planned with the intention of relocating both jobs and housing from city centers. However, the population density in city centers has not been decreased in reality. Instead, those suburban areas with inadequate mixed-used development have gradually been connected to cities centers, leading to urban sprawl. This is compounded by wide roads but inadequate multimodal transport and local roads and insufficient proper public transit connections. As a result, traffic has become concentrated on arterial roads and expressways that link city centers and their suburban areas, thus causing higher levels of car dependency, traffic congestion, excessive consumption of

[1]   UN-Habitat, *State of China's Cities 2010/2011: Better City, Better Life*, 2010, Foreign Languages Press.

[2]   Wang, J. and He, D., "Sustainable Urban Development in China: Challenges and Achievements", *Mitigation and Adaptation Strategies for Global Change*, 20, 2015, pp. 665 – 682.

energy and other urban challenges.

Policy and decision makers in China have increasingly recognized and paid great attention to the challenges and their negative implications. Various strategies/approaches have been adopted to tackle the challenges, which are reflected in major events that have been taken place and policies on environmental protection and sustainable development that have been issued to tackle the challenges caused by the rapid urbanization process in the country. For instance, environmental protection was identified by the State Council as a national strategy at the Second National Environmental Protection Working Meeting in 1983. The State Council issued the *Ten Major Measures for China's Environmental Protection and Development* in 1992, which are specific approaches related to sustainable development in China. Sustainable development was set as a national strategy for modernization at the Fifteenth National Congress of the CPC in 1997. The concept of *Ecological Civilization* was proposed at the Seventeenth National Congress of the CPC in 2007, which is related to both environmental protection and sustainable development. In 2015, the amendments to the *Environmental Protection Law of the People's Republic of China* came into force in 2015, which assign more responsibilities to enterprises for pollution prevention, impose harsher penalties for environmental pollution and establish the environmental public interest litigation system. The following is a summary of major events and policies on environmental protection and sustainable development in China since 1970s.

Table 1   Major Events and Policies on Environmental Protection and Sustainable Development in China since 1970s

Year	Policy/Policies	Event/Issuing Authority	Main Points/Significance
1973	*Decisions of the State Council on Issues Concerning Environmental Protection and Improvement*	First National Environmental Protection Working Meeting held by the SPC entrusted by the State Council	The *Decisions* identifies principles related to planning, utilization of resources and public participation in environment protection, which marks the beginning of environment protection in contemporary China.
1979	*Environmental Protection Law of the People's Republic of China* (*on trial*)	SCNPC	It is the first law on environmental protection in the People's Republic of China, which was formulated based on the *Constitution of the People's Republic of China* (Amended in 1978).
1982	*Constitution of the People's Republic of China* (*Amended in 1982*)	NPC	It is the first time that environmental protection, pollution prevention and control as well as natural resources conservation were written in the *Constitution*, the most fundamental law in the People's Republic of China.

Cont.

Year	Policy/Policies	Event/Issuing Authority	Main Points/Significance
1982	*Sixth Five-Year Plan for National Economic and Social Development*	State Council	The *Plan* has a separate chapter on environmental protection, which identifies environmental protection as one of the ten major tasks facing the government.
1983		Second National Environmental Protection Working Meeting held by the State Council	The Meeting identifies environmental protection as national strategy, which greatly raises public awareness of environmental protection, and formulates general guidelines on environmental protection in China that suits the country.
1989	*Environmental Protection Objectives and Tasks* (1989 – 1992); and *Outline of the National Environmental Protection Plan Towards* 2000	Third National Environmental Protection Working Meeting held by the State Council	The Meeting evaluates current situations of environmental protection in China, summarizes the successful experience gained from the three environmental management systems; and proposes additional five systems and measures, which constitute the "Eight Environmental Management Systems" in China.
1989	*Environmental Protection Law of the People's Republic of China* (*Amended in* 1989)	SCNPC	The amended Law includes the above-mentioned systems, which strengthens legal basis for environmental protection.
1992	*Ten Major Measures for China's Environmental Protection and Development*	State Council	These are specific measures related to sustainable development in China. It is a guiding document on China's environmental protection and development.

Cont.

Year	Policy/Policies	Event/Issuing Authority	Main Points/Significance
1994	*China's Agenda 21: White Paper on Population, Environment and Development in the 21st Century*	State Council	The *China's Agenda* 21 proposes that the objectives and contents mentioned in this policy should be integrated into the national economic and social development plans and long-term plans. It is a significant starting point to integrate the concept and objectives of sustainable development into policy-making process at the national level in China.
1996	*Decisions of the State Council on Issues Concerning Environmental Protection*	Fourth National Environmental Protection Working Meeting held by the State Council	The *Decisions* identifies environmental protection as the most important task in the sustainable development strategy. It starts a new chapter for environmental protection in China.
1996	*National Environmental Protection Plan during the Ninth Five-year Plan Period; and Vision 2010*	SEPA	They are guiding documents on environment protection for the five-year plan period from 1996 to 2000 and the following fifteen years up to 2010.
1997		Fifteenth National Congress of the CPC	Sustainable development was set as a national strategy for modernization.
2001	*National Environmental Protection Plan during the Tenth Five-year Plan Period*	SEPA	The policy contains the *Plan for Controlling the Total Emission of Major Pollutants* and *Plan for Green Engineering Program (Phase II)*. It is the guiding document on environmental protection for the five-year plan period from 2001 to 2005.

Cont.

Year	Policy/Policies	Event/Issuing Authority	Main Points/Significance
2002		Fifth National Environmental Protection Working Meeting held by the State Council	The *Meeting* makes arrangements for the implementation of the *National Environmental Protection Plan during the Tenth Five-year Plan* Period. It points out that environmental protection is a significant function of the government who intends to mobilize the whole country to protect the environment.
2003	*Environmental Impact Assessment Law of the People's Republic of China*	SCNPC	The *Law* intends to prevent negative impacts on the environment due to the implementation of various plans and construction projects to achieve sustainable development. It is a significant legal basis for implementing the sustainable development strategy.
2005	*National Environmental Protection Plan during the Eleventh Five-year Plan Period*	SEPA and NDRC	The policy is the guiding document on environmental protection for the five-year plan period from 2006 to 2010.
2006	*Methods on Punishment for Violations of Environmental Protection Laws and Regulations* (*on trial*)	MoS and SEPA	The *Methods* intends to promote the implementation of environmental protection laws and regulations by penalizing violations. It is a significant policy to strengthen environmental protection and management.

Cont.

Year	Policy/Policies	Event/Issuing Authority	Main Points/Significance
2006		Sixth National Environmental Protection Working Meeting held by the State Council	The Meeting proposes " Three Shifts" in the attitudes towards environmental protection and management by shifting the previous attitudes to: the same emphasis placed on environmental protection and economic growth; the same pace of environmental protection and economic development; and utilizing a comprehensive method, such as legal, economic, technological and administrative means (only when necessary) to deal with environmental issues. The "Three Shifts" is significant to achieve environmental objectives in the new era of environmental protection.
2007	*Report to the Seventeenth National Congress of the Communist Party of China*	Seventeenth National Congress of the CPC	The *Report* officially proposes the concept of " Ecological Civilization". The Concept relates to both environmental protection and sustainable development.
2007	*Methods on Public Release of Environmental Information (on trial)*	SEPA	The *Methods* intends to standardize the disclosure of environmental information to the public. It is an important policy to encourage public participation in environmental protection.

Cont.

Year	Policy/Policies	Event/Issuing Authority	Main Points/Significance
2011	*Suggestions of the State Council on Promoting Environmental Protection*	Seventh National Environmental Protection Working Meeting held by the State Council	The Meeting emphasizes effective implementation by ways such as improving environmental protection management, strengthening supervision over environmental law enforcement, etc.
2011	*Twelfth Five-year Plan for National Environmental Protection*	MEP	It is a guiding document on environmental protection for the five-year plan period from 2011 to 2015.
2014	*Environmental Protection Law of the People's Republic of China (Amended in 2014)*	SCNPC	It is the most updated law on environmental protection, which was enforced on 1 January 2015.
2016	*Thirteenth Five-Year Plan for National Eco-environmental Conservation*	MEP	It is a guiding document on eco-environmental conservation for the five-year plan period from 2016 to 2020.

Source: Own analysis and summary.

In line with sustainable development, *sustainable urbanization* was suggested by UN-Habitat/DFID as an important component in 2002, which is characterized by the urbanization process that fulfills the principles of sustainable development[1]. Sustainable urbanization

---

① UN-Habitat/DFID, Sustainable Urbanization: Achieving Agenda 21, 2002, United Nations Human Settlement Programme/Department for International Development.

is an effective way to achieve sustainable urban development in China, which is conducive to tackling the above-mentioned urban challenges caused by rapid urbanization process[1]. A joint research conducted by World Bank and DRC in 2014 suggested that China needs to transform from its traditional model to the *New Model of Urbanization* that is more efficient, inclusive and sustainable. Here, " *Efficient Urbanization* makes the best possible use of China's productive resources: its people, land, and capital; *Inclusive Urbanization* provides all people access to equal opportunity to benefit from urbanization—to use their labor where they are most productive, to accumulate assets and savings, and to use public services of similar quality across China; and *Sustainable Urbanization* means urbanization that can be supported by China's environment (land, air, water) and natural resources, while providing an urban quality of life commensurate with the desires of China's people"[2].

---

[1]   Tan, Y. , Xu, H. and Zhang, X. , Sustainable Urbanization in China: A Comprehensive Literature Review, *Cities*, 55, 2016, pp. 82 – 93; Zhao, P. , Sustainable Urban Expansion and Transportation in a Growing Megacity: Consequences of Urban Sprawl for Mobility on the Urban Fringe of Beijing, *Habitat International*, 34 (2), 2010, pp. 236 – 243.

[2]   World Bank and DRC, Urban China: Toward Efficient, Inclusive, and Sustainable Urbanization, 2014.

The concept of the *New-Type Urbanization with Chinese Characteristics* (hereinafter referred to as the " *New-Type Urbanization*") was proposed in the *Decision of the CCCPC on Some Major Issues Concerning Comprehensively Deepening the Reform* (hereinafter referred to as the "*Decision*") adopted at the Third Plenary Session of the 18th Central Committee of the Communist Party of China in 2013[①]. The *Decision* advocates the improvement of institutions and mechanisms for a sound process of urbanization in China, which emphasizes people-entered urbanization; the coordinated development between large, median-sized and small cities as well as towns; the industry-and-city integration; and the coordinated development between urban and new rural areas in the process of urbanization. The *Decision* also advocates the optimization of urban spatial structure and urban management and the expansion of urban carrying capacity. The *New-Type Urbanization* takes into full consideration China's national circumstances and the necessity of its transformation from the traditional to a more scientific way of development in the process of

---

① http: //www. china. org. cn/chinese/2014 – 01/17/content_ 31226494. htm.

rapid urbanization[1], which reflects the concepts of *sustainable urbanization and New Model of Urbanization.*

Numerous pilot projects have been implemented in areas in relation to the *New-Type Urbanization*, such as more compact and mixed-use development, more efficient energy use and waste management, etc. A few pilot projects that have become good practices are being scaled up, which can help tackle the urban challenges across the country. In the following chapter, selected good practices in China will be illustrated according to the six themes, Sustainable Urban Planning and Management, Energy Efficiency and Low-carbon Development, Transport and Mobility, Urban Renewal and Municipal Solid Waste Management, Sharing Economy and the Contribution of Private Sectors and Smart Urban Governance.

[1]   Qiu B, Q. , On the New of the New Type of Urbanization, 2016.

Chapter Three

Good Practices in Europe and China

1. Sustainable Urban Planning and Urban Renewal

1. 1. Overview

People centred urban planning and the renewal of the existing housing stock towards energy efficiency and for enhancing the quality of life of the residents are key to sustainable urban development. To this end, the example of the project SubUrbanLab show cases how co-design in urban living labs and participatory planning can modernize and socially uplift underprivileged neighbourhoods. In Chinese cities, the development of superblocks has hindered the walkability in urban areas and contributed to urban sprawl. The large-scale renewal project in Nanchong Prefecture (Sichuan

Province) illustrates how urban planning and renewal can contribute to the human scale developments by promoting a multi-centric urban structure and thus enhance walkability, access to public parks and thus contribute to sustainable and liveable urban areas.

1. 2. Case Studies in Europe

JPI UE Project: SubUrbanLab

Suburban Lab aims to examine how municipal authorities can engage with local residents and other stakeholders, and how they can work together to modernize and socially uplift underprivileged neighbourhoods and suburbs and turn these suburbs into more attractive, sustainable and economically viable urban areas. The project sets up urban living labs in two suburbs in Sweden and Finland as a mean to develop new forms of actively involving residents and stakeholders in shaping their own urban contexts.

Ⅰ. Stakeholder involvement in upgrading of local areas

Across Europe, some 200 million people live in suburbs containing large scale housing areas in great need of modernization and social uplifting. These areas are less valued in the sense that they usually have large-scale architecture and the local environments are commonly seen as less attractive and amongst the residents, the majority is socially and economically underprivileged.

In Sweden and Finland these types of areas have been the subject of recurrent governmental initiatives and reform programs aimed at improving public spaces, improving the energy efficiency of buildings, improving waste management and to support social cohesion and trust in the local public authorities by way of engaging local residents in local processes. Piloting and testing solutions is becoming a more common feature in selected approaches.

Ⅱ. Urban living labs

The Suburban Lab project, was carried out between 2014 – 2016, by VTT Technical Research Centre of Finland and IVL Swedish Environmental Research institute in cooperation with Botkyrka Municipality in Sweden and the City of Riihimäki, Finland. The project developed and set up in total six Urban Living Labs (ULLs) in Sweden and Finland.

Urban living labs (ULLs) utilize various co-design methods for understanding stakeholders needs, generating and presenting ideas and evaluating the solutions in practice. It is a forum for innovation which develops new products, systems, services, and processes for urban areas. Urban living labs employ methods which put people at the heart of the entire development process as both users and co-creators. They allow people to test, explore, examine, experiment with and evaluate new ideas to come up with creative solutions in complex every day contexts. Nearly half of the 67 projects financed in JPI Urban Europe calls since 2012 includes elements of ULLs and there is now a substantial portfolio of projects that test urban living labs in different settings and contexts.

This project examined how the urban living lab approach could be used to actively involve the residents and other stakeholders in two suburbs, Alby in Sweden and Riihimäki in Finland, in the modernization and social uplifting of their suburbs and local neighbourhoods, co-developing and testing new services or solutions in their daily life. Users of the new services or solutions were active partners in the whole development process which took place in their real urban contexts. The descriptions below of two of the urban living labs illustrates how the project focused on relatively modest and small-scale projects that provides opportunities for collaboration.

"New light on Alby Hill" focused on how to transform a walkway so that it was both more attractive and safer. Ambient lighting and light installations along the walkway were planned, designed and implemented together with researchers, public organizations, companies, non-governmental organizations and

Vote for your favorite image!

Nytt ljus på Albyberget

During the autumn we asked for images to be used for lightening up stonewalls along a walkway on Albyberget. 20 images were submitted and we have chosen six to be part of the final voting. The two winning images will light up one stonewall each. **Vote for YOUR favorite image now!**

 You can vote by using the QR-code or via the website **www.nyttljus.eu**

You can vote until the 8th of March.

1. Peace – Brandy Contreras Sanchez and Oulaymatou Jallow

2. Alby i mitt hjärta – Jannika Ojeda Meftah

3. Nej till rasism – Jasmine Icke

4. Höghus – Lema Murad

5. Vi är lika – Tamona

6. Vårt Alby – Mirac Yavuz och Rami Khalil

SubUrbanLab MITT ALBY URBAN•EUROPE Svenska Miljöinstitutet

Ett samarbete

"Nytt Ljus på Albyberget" är ett samarbete mellan Botkyrka kommun, Mitt Alby AB, Konstfack och IVL Svenska Miljöinstitutet. "Nytt ljus på Albyberget" är en del av projektet SubUrbanLab (suburbanlab.eu), och arbetet utför med bidrag från Vinnova inom ramen för JPI Urban Europe, och är det andra av tre Urban Living Lab (ULL) som kommer att genomföras i Alby.

Figure 5   Poster from the urban living lab "New light on Alby Hill"

residents, who also suggested images for the light installations under the theme of "Our Alby". The winning images were chosen through open voting. Contributions to social and environmental sustainability increased the sense of security, laying the foundation for continued participation among residents, whilst achieving aims such as decreasing the energy use of the street lightning.

"Together more" in Peltosaari, provided residents with accessible opportunities to participate in the planning and development of their environment and arranging local activities. The goal was to improve the appreciation of the area and to increase communal feelings among the residents. Several types of activities were piloted and residents were engaged in discussions about plans concerning the area. The project piloted new kinds of events which also managed to reach young people in the area and enhanced collaboration between various groups. The area gained a lot of positive press coverage.

Ⅲ. Key success factors, main experiences and lessons learnt from six Urban Living Labs

The key success factors for Urban Living Labs are the early and continuous involvement of the people affected by them, having clear goals and expectations, and acting instead of simply discussing.

The methods must be adapted to the goals and to the participants. At its best, people can participate in the Urban Living Lab activities as a part of their other activities and see the effects of their participation shortly afterwards.

Experiences from the six urban living labs stress amongst other things that each Urban Living Lab was shaped and changed along the way as a consequence of the context of where it was set, and by unexpected events and the impact from different stakeholders. Processes were not linear—they took unexpected turns as researchers, decision-makers and public organizations, residents and companies took part in the co-creation of each Urban Living Lab.

Lessons learnt from the project include insights on how to best encourage engagement from local residents on the one hand and the municipality on the other hand. The project also showed how user-driven urban living labs, primarily run by the residents, may further strengthen residents' feelings of inclusion and participation in the local society, while an enabler-driven urban living lab, run by the municipality, may increase the chances of sufficient resources if the working methods of living labs are fully embraced and integrated into existing organizational routines.

Ⅳ. Boundary conditions and guidance to cities

Elements and boundary conditions that need to be taken into consideration when setting up urban living labs have been identified through literature reviews and interviews with residents on their past experiences of stakeholder involvement. Boundary conditions for Urban Living Labs are presented as checklists with questions for each of the five elements (see Figure 6) , that should be answered before starting ULL activities and practical examples and recommendations for answering the questions.

"The most important outcome from the project Suburban Lab was the fact that we could identify (generally applicable) boundary conditions and key success factors for Urban Living Labs, that can be used to give clear guidance to other cities on how to set up similar living labs. The methods are replicable in other cities but the themes for the Urban Living Labs have to be defined based on the city-specific needs", says Riikka Holopainen, research Team Leader, D. Sc. (Tech) at VTT Technical Research Centre of Finland. Riikka Holopainen continues by saying " The local stakeholders involved in the project in Alby and Riihimäki benefitted from the project in terms of more sustainability in their local environments and everyday life" .

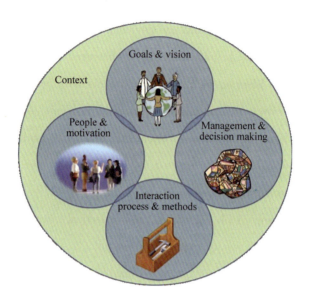

Figure 6　Five elements of planning an Urban Living Lab

Source: Bäck et al. , 2012.

V. Booklets and guidelines[1]

The booklet "Urban Living Labs as arenas for co-creation in urban areas" describing success factors together and lessons learned and the report "Boundary conditions for successful Urban Living Labs"[2] are targeting organizations who want to start and lead urban

---

① http: //suburbanlab. eu/wp-content/uploads/2016/05/SubUrbanLab_ booklet_ screen. pdf.

② http: //suburbanlab. eu/tulokset/? lang = en.

living labs in connection to modernization and uplifting actions.

SubUrbanLab: Social uplifting and modernization of suburban areas with Urban Living Lab approach

Duration: 2013 – 2016

Internet: www. jpi-urbaneurope. eu/suburbanlab

Contact: Riikka Holopainen, VTT Technical Research Centre of Finland Ltd.

E-mail: riikka. holopainen@ vtt. fi

Partners: IVL Swedish Environmental Research institute, Botkyrka Municipality, City of Riihimäki, VTT Technical Research Centre of Finland Ltd.

---

1. 3. **Case Studies in China**

The development of superblocks in Chinese cities mentioned in the previous chapter has contributed greatly to pedestrian-unfriendly built environments and traffic congestion. More compact and mixed-use development could help reduce urban sprawl and car dependency as well as increase walkability and efficiency in infrastructure and services distribution and delivery.

Several pilot projects are making efforts to develop smaller-grid street networks, such as a the Caofeidian International Eco-City and the Tianjin Sino-Singapore Eco-city (see Figure 7). Themain features of the latter include " transit-oriented development, mixed land use, eco-recovery, large eco land use and zero wetland lose, renewable energy, intelligent grid, untraditional water treatment and reuse, cleaning and utilization of garbage, green transportation and fuel, green building and eco-industry park"[1].

Figure 7   The Street Networks in Tianjin Sino-Singapore Eco-city
Source: Google Earth.

However, the grids are still large in Chinese eco-cities

① Wang, J. and He, D. , Sustainable Urban Development in China: Challenges and Achievements, *Mifigation and Adaptation Strategies for Global Change*, 20, 2015, pp. 665 – 682.

compared to those in Europe, such as the eco-city in Barcelona, Spain. Figure 8 compares the proposed human-scale street networks between the eco-city of Caofeidian in China and that of Barcelona in Spain.

Figure 8   A Comparison of the Proposed Human-scale Street Networks between the Eco-City of Caofeidian in China (Left) and that of Barcelona in Spain (Right)

Source: Wang, J. and He, D., "Sustainable Urban Development in China: Challenges and Achievements", *Mitigation and Adaptation Strategies for Global Change*, 20, 2015, pp. 665 – 682.

One approach to reducing the grid is to incorporate the micro-scale into the existing macro-scale development by redeveloping brownfields for mixed-use development and increasing accessibility and greenspaces. Figure 9 are conceptual diagrams showing how coarse grids can be refined by applying the above-mentioned approach. In the diagram on the left, the pink polygon represents one of the mono-functional and car-oriented grids that are pedestrian-unfriendly. The coarse grids are refined by adding public transport networks and green corridors to the existing coarse grids (see the diagram on the right). These can be refined further with networks for bikes and pedestrians.

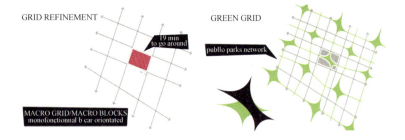

Figure 9   Conceptual Diagrams of the Approach: Incorporating the
Micro-scale into the Existing Macro-scale Development

Source: http://www.inktalks.com/discover/691/neville-mars-urban-renewal-of-
mumbai-and-china.

Consequently, the massive plots of the coarse grids can be

refined to human scale from the perspective of land use (see Figure 10), which may increase diversity and enhance resilience overtime, thus conducive to sustainable urban development. These refined grids can feed into the existing urban areas, which contributes to the solving of the urban challenges caused by the development of superblocks and urban sprawls. The following is a case study of Nanchong prefecture in China.

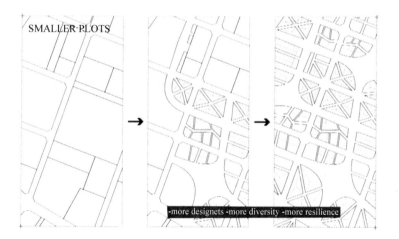

Figure 10   Potential Effects of Applying the Approach:
More Diversity and Resilience

Source: http://www.inktalks.com/discover/691/neville-mars-urban-renewal-of-mumbai-and-china.

1. 4. Case Study: Nanchong Prefecture, Sichuan Province

Nanchong is a prefecture-level city located in the middle reaches of Jialing River and the northeast of Sichuan Province, China. The prefecture governs three urban districts, one city and five counties[1] within its jurisdiction, with an area of 12, 500 square kilometres and population of 7. 6 million[2]. There are 126 square kilometres and 1. 25 million population in its three urban districts, i. e. Shunqing District, Gaoping District and Jialing District in 2017[3].

A large-scale urban renewal project was launched in Nanchong in 2009, which involves 1. 65 million square meters, with 3, 000 households being relocated. The project retrofitted historic buildings, leaving a nostalgic legacy to its residents[4]. The prefecture's built environment and ecological environment have been changed dramatically with its economic and transportation development in recent years (see Figure 11 and Figure 12).

---

[1] Shunqing District, Gaoping District, Jialing District, Langzhong City (a county-level city), Nanbu County, Yingshan County, Peng'an County, Yilong County and Xichong County.

[2] http: //www. nanchong. gov. cn/10000/10004/10007/10030/2016/03/08/10127357. shtml.

[3] Ibid. .

[4] http: //nc. newssc. org/system/20161116/002057336_ 2. html.

Figure 11   The Road, Bus Lane and Pedestrian Networks in the

Transport Plan for Upgrading the Networks in the Urban Districts

of Nanchong Prefecture

Source: http://www.nanchong.gov.cn/10000/10003/10211/2015/03/06/1011

8318.shtml.

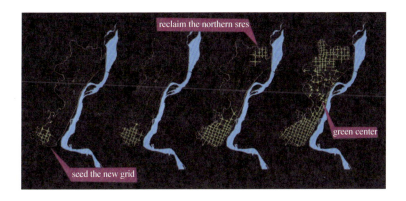

Figure 12   The Gradual Incorporation of the Micro-scale into the

Existing Macro-scale Development in Shunqing and Jialing

Districts in Nanchong Prefecture

Source: http://www.inktalks.com/discover/691/neville-mars-urban-renewal-of-

mumbai-and-china.

The development of individual business centers in Gaoping and Jialing Districts in addition to their higher population density and the development of road networks and industries give rise to a multi-centric urban structure of the prefecture. This is conducive to its sustainable socio-economic development, with statistics for Gross Regional Product, disposable income of urban residents and urban population pointing to steady increase in the decade from 2006 to 2015.

With the development of the multi-centric structure, urban recreation centers have been expanded to develop and include more public parks (e. g. , Xihe Sports Park, Nanmenba Ecological Park and Baita Park) and pedestrian networks in Nanchong. This has gradually incorporated the micro-scale into the existing macro-scale development, which increases walkability and access to public parks, thus beneficial for residents and sustainable urban development of Nanchong.

2. Energy Efficiency and Low-carbon Development

2. 1. Overview

Urban areas have great potential to reduce greenhouse gas

emissions and increase energy efficiency, thus contributing to actions of climate change mitigation. This does not only require renewable energy technologies or innovative energy management but also changing user behaviours. In this sense, the project me^2 aims at creating a community platform to increase awareness of the energy consumption among citizens and investigate ways to change user behaviours towards greater energy efficiency. The me^2 concept was tested in two Urban Living Labs in Amsterdam (the Netherlands) and Lisbon (Portugal). In China, efforts have been made on policy level. Several Chinese ministries have promoted sustainable urban development by launching eco-cities policies, standards and pilot programmes for low carbon development. One of the best cases in China, Hangzhou City, followed an ambitious plan to become a low-carbon city and a role model for sustainable development countrywide.

2.2. Case Study in Europe

JPI UE Project: me^2

The project highlights include the pilots in Amsterdam and Lisbon, the policy analysis and survey results as well as the me^2 platform. The project applies smart grids, electric mobility, business models and policy incentives to the development of an innovative service concept.

The goal of me^2 is to make citizens more aware of energy consumption, incentivise changes in their individual and collective behaviour to save on electricity costs, while being connected with a local community. The concept has been validated and optimized in two practical pilots in urban communities in Amsterdam and Lisbon. me^2 affects consumers, utility companies, grid operators, electricity suppliers, municipalities, and car sharing companies.

"Throughout me^2 there has been continuous development and we have been adjusting things and fine-tuning it the whole time" says Halldora Thorsdottir, me^2 project manager and researcher at the Urban Technology research programme of the Amsterdam University of Applied Sciences.

The combination of data technologies in a community allows the integration of mobility with electricity, to balance the grid, to reduce electricity costs, and to enable a feeling of local belonging. me^2 enables urban demand-side management, i. e. aims to modify consumer demand for energy such as using less energy during peak hours in an urban community.

"One of the motivations was to bring together the increasing significance of electric vehicles and smart grids. All of the project's pilot participants got a smart meter, but we were particularly interested in the role that EVs (electric vehicles) play. The participants have a house but, especially in the Netherlands, also an EV and charging point, and some have solar panels", says Halldora Thorsdottir.

One of the developments that me^2 is based on is the fact that homes and small-scale businesses are becoming small energy producers with the potential to provide a solution to managing peak demand and grid balancing. 75% of the Dutch participants own a private charging point and a little over half of the households produce renewable electricity using PV installations. This is important as such initiatives and ventures are expected to be an integral part of the future EU energy system management.

"The project creates a new market place for urban actors in which a local community of electric vehicle (EV) users and local smart meter (SM) owners are brought together in an urban online community", says Wolfgang Prüggler, CEO of Moosmoar Energies OG (MME), one of the project partners.

I . Pilots in Lisbon and Amsterdam

The target of the pilots has been to test the quality and experience of the me^2 integrated energy monitoring platform. The first pilot was in Lisbon with 50 people taking part in a closed community system. The project used several devices in order to track energy consumption: smart plugs for home consumption and charging and MOBI-E plugs for public charging. The Dutch pilot involved 50 households in an open system with private electric vehicles. This pilot differs from the Lisbon pilot as the number of EV users was higher. This is due to the Netherlands having one of the highest percentages of electric vehicles in Europe. The participants in both countries installed smart meters and opened me[2]

Figure 13　Via me[2] accounts and personal dashboards consumers have access directly to their energy information laying the base for mechanisms to influence behavior

accounts, so that their energy usage could be collected and they could see it on a personal dashboard.

Ⅱ. Gamification

Gamification was key to our success. Before the pilot it became clear in a cross-cultural analysis that the social aspect and gamification is more important in the Netherlands, whilst in Portugal the participants were not motivated by competition but instead very motivated by self-improvement and helping the environment.

"In both pilots we gave incentives to the users on how to reduce energy usage and how to handle peak hour consumption. In Portugal these were mainly focused on financial and environmental arguments. In the Netherlands we focused on social comparison and gamification. Our user community consisted of people trying to do their best, they were highly interested in technological and efficiency related details, and they wanted to play the game against themselves to see how they could perform. They are perhaps less interested in the savings they make in return, it is more the case that they want to do good", says Halldora Thorsdottir.

In Portugal the users would get points every week for reducing energy usage. In the Dutch pilot a similar algorithm was introduced and used at peak hours, between 5: 00 and 9: 00 in the evening, with users getting additional points and getting a message about it which stated "You have reduced your consumption!" and a ranking where they could see how they were doing with the winner getting a prize. The first phase resulted in a white book report in which recommendations for the different phases of user interaction are given, along with an evaluation of the effects of the incentives in the two project pilot cities along with practical findings. One of the lessons learned from having a technical pilot is that even though the devices are "plug and play" people are not used to them and tend to say they will do it tomorrow.

It's a complex project with many different facets, the technical part is quite important and complicated and then there's the social part in setting up a pilot, "it took a long time to get it altogether, to realize the most important components for success" explains Halldora when reflecting on the two year project period.

Ⅲ. Platform and App

The me^2 integrated energy monitoring platform is the front end of the project's Smart City Aggregator (SCA) system. The SCA connects use of EV batteries and households' equipment with smart meters, to achieve greater efficiency and flexibility at an electricity grid level or the back end. The front end includes a community website, an app and an intelligent back end. The consumers have access directly to their energy information laying the base for mechanisms to influence behavior. The app is available for iOS and Android and serves to increase the accessibility of the platform. Users can share their results, if for example they have acquired green points and other users can "like" what they are doing.

Figure 14   The web-based platform shows consumption by appliance, locality or categories like heating or cooling on a dashboard

At the back-end of the smart city aggregator we can have utilities or different companies that gather all the profiles of the consumers on the front end. The front end has been tested in the pilots which gave us feedback for further development. This can also become an interesting product for an energy provider or for a company that is allowed to trade on the energy market. Halldora Thorsdottir argues "You can optimize the management and use of energy".

The data from the smart meters was sent to the me^2 platform. The web-based platform shows consumption by appliance, locality or categories like heating or cooling. The collected data have been compared with results from a pre-pilot survey asking the participants about their consumption. A user scenario has also been developed. The technical partner, MediaPrimer, has been engaged from the beginning and has put a lot of effort in making the front-end; the website, the app and the platform. The aggregator can communicate directly with the users through the platform and has the means to send messages to consumers such as "the peak hour is costly for you to load your car, it's better to do it later" or "if you charge it at different time you get more points".

In addition, the market square, an online market place of me^2 and connected to the platform, was developed by our other technical partner, VPS. The idea is that companies that have energy efficiency service, for example solar panels or other smart tools or services that facilitate smart charging of electric vehicles as affiliated partners will be on the market square. The users can go there and see if the products are enticing. There are now several ideas on how to take the outcomes to the next step.

Our commercial partners are now focusing on exactly what the next step should be. Halldora says "in principal they want to take the product further, they are participating in an active discussion on research, testing and development before finding the best way to take it to the market."

Ⅳ. When will smart solutions like the smart meter be standard

It's already happening. I think in the Netherlands more and more people want to know if they can save energy, our users for example really want to see all of their production and consumption in one place and in the platform you see everything. This is something that we are offering in me^2, and this is also what other smart home solutions will offer, and some are already doing it Halldora Thorsdottir concludes the future prospects.

---

me^2: Integrated smart city mobility and energy platform

Duration: 2016 – 2018

Internet: www. jpi-urbaneurope. eu/me2

Contact: Dr. Robert van den Hoed, Amsterdam University of Applied Sciences

E-mail: r. van. den. hoed@ hva. nl

Partners: Amsterdam University of Applied Sciences, UCP Católica Lisbon School of Business & Economics, Lisboa E-NOVA, Agência Municipal De Energia-Ambiente De Lisboa, MOOSMOAR Energies, Virtual Power Solutions, MediaPrimer

Acknowledgement: This project has received funding from the European Union's Horizon 2020 research and innovation programme under grant agreement No 646453.

2. 3. Case Study in China

Cities around the world generate 80% of GDP, according to recent estimates[1]. Meanwhile, they are responsible for approximately 70% of global energy-related GHG emissions, which imposes an additional challenge for Chinese cities, given that China has been the largest contributor of carbon emissions in recent years[2].

Figure 15 shows CO_2 emissions by Sector from 1990 to 2009 in China. Based on an estimate by the International Energy Agency (IEA), emissions by the electricity and heat generation sector had increased significantly since 1990, accounting for approximately 50% of all emissions in 2007[3]. In 2013, China remitted about

---

① Dobbs, R. et al. , Urban world/Mapping the Economic Power of Cities, 2011.
② World Bank, Sustainable Low-Carbon City Development in China, 2012.
③ OECD/IEA, CO2 Emissions from Fuel Combustion 2011, 2009, Paris, France: OECD/IEA.

25% of carbon dioxide in the world, i. e. 9. 2 Gt CO_2; 73% of the increase in global carbon emissions between 2010 and 2012 occurred in China; without mitigation, the emissions in the county could rise by over 50% in the next 15 years[1]. CO_2 emissions would continue to grow quickly across all key sectors unless effective measures were implemented to lower carbon intensity.

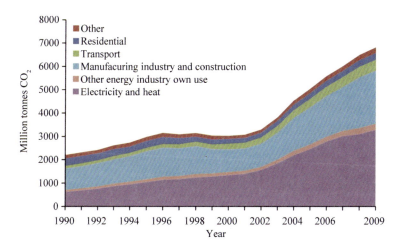

Figure 15 CO_2 Emissions by Sector in China (1990 – 2009)

Source: OECD/IEA, 2011.

---

① Zhu, L. , China's Carbon Emissions Report: 2016—Regional Carbon Emissions and the Implication for China's Low Carbon Development, 2016.

Fortunately, policy makers, over the last decades, have recognized the need for reducing carbon emissions and energy use while maintaining robust economic growth to create more employment opportunities and improve people's quality of life. Since early 1990s, The Ministry of Environmental Protection (MEP) and the Ministry of Housing and Urban-Rural Development (MoHURD) have attempted to guide cities towards more sustainable development by ways including releasing various eco-city policies and standards. By 2012, MEP had designated 11 counties, districts, and cities as eco-cities, i. e. Miyun county and Yanqing county in Beijing; Taicang city, Zhangjiagang city, Changshu city and Jiangyin city in Jiangsu province; Rongcheng city in Shandong province; Yantian district in Shenzhen; Minhang district in Shanghai; and Anji county in Zhejiang province. MoHURD's National Eco-Garden Cities include Shenzen, Qingdao, Nanjing, Hangzhou, Weihai, Yangzhou, Suzhou, Shaoxing, Guilin, Changshu, Kunshan and Zhangjiagang.

Apart from MEP and MoHURD, the National Development and Reform Commission (NDRC) launched a pilot program for national low-carbon province and city development in 2010. The program has been implemented in five provinces (Guangdong, Liaoning,

Hubei, Shaanxi, and Yunnan) and eight cities or municipalities (Tianjin, Chongqing, Shenzhen, Xiamen, Hangzhou, Nanchang, Guiyang and Baoding) across the country.

Although some local governments may still have inadequate capacity to transform themselves to low-carbon cities, the pilot programs mentioned above have positive impacts on the determination of local governments' striving for low-carbon development. One positive side in practice is that the increase in energy efficiency and the achievement of low-carbon development in Chinese cities are in line with sustainable urban development in the context of the rapid urbanization process. Cities that engage in low-carbon transformation will become more livable, efficient, resilient, and ultimately more sustainable.

There are emerging Low-Carbon City Initiatives in cities such as Shenzhen, Wuxi, Guiyang, Baoding and Hangzhou. Some of these initiatives appear similar in nature to the previous generation of eco-cities, thus sharing similar achievements and shortcomings. Low-carbon development in Hangzhou represents a good practice among them.

2.4. Case Study: Low-carbon Development in Hangzhou City[1]

Hangzhou, capital of Zhejiang province, is located in eastern coast of China, with the population 9.188 million, population density of 554 persons per square kilometer and an area of 16,596 square kilometers by the end of 2016[2]. It is the first city in China who proposed the low-carbon city strategy (in 2008), aiming to reduce its carbon intensity by 35% by 2015 and 50% by 2020 against a 2005 baseline.

In 2009, Hangzhou released *the Decision on Low-Carbon City Development*, with an intension to transform itself to a low-carbon city and become a role model for low-carbon development in China. It proposed the development of a low-carbon demonstration city after it was identified by NDRC as one of the first Low-carbon Pilot Cities in the country, with a special focus on the following six themes, i.e. low-carbon economy, low-carbon transport, low-carbon buildings, low-carbon living, low-carbon energy and low-carbon

---

① http://district.ce.cn/zg/201508/25/t20150825_6311730.shtml; http://hznews.hangzhou.com.cn/jingji/content/2016-10/28/content_6363947.htm; World Bank, Sustainable Low-Carbon City Development in China, 2012.

② http://tjj.hangzhou.gov.cn/web/tjnj/nj2017/index.htm.

society.

Since then, Hangzhou has adopted various initiatives. For the development of low-carbon economy, it has emphasized structural transformation and industrial upgrading by phasing out high-polluting and high-energy consumption businesses, and meanwhile, encouraging the development of cleaner production and circular economy. The city has established a comprehensive low-carbon public transport system, which consists of a public bicycle system, electric taxi services, a low-carbon bus scheme, water bus services and a metro system. By the end of 2015, there were 1,230 electric buses, 560 electric buses, 2,378 LNG buses and 3,866 CNG taxis in operation; the city became well known for its world largest public bicycle system, with 80,000 public bicycles and over 3,000 docking stations distributed in its city center and more than 400 million bike rides. Energy saving technologies have been applied to existing and new buildings to increase energy efficiency and reduce carbon emissions in the city. This includes, but is not limited to, encouraging the development of photovoltaic power generations, green rooftops and vertical greenery, and implementing the Green Building Rating System.

The above-mentioned initiatives and practices in Hangzhou

have accomplished tremendous achievements. In 2015, the total coal consumption of the city was reduced by over 6% compared to that of 2012; clean coal utilization rate reached over 80%; renewable energy accounted for around 4% of total energy consumption. By the end of 2015, the unit GDP energy consumption was reduced to 0.43 ton of standard coal/10, 000 yuan, a drop by 23.25% against a 2010 baseline, which exceeded the goal of the reduction by 19.5% set for the Twelfth Five-year Plan period.

3. Transport and Mobility

3.1. Overview

Efforts are taken worldwide to improve mobility systems with the aim to provide safe access for all people to public places, goods, services and economic opportunities, while at the same time reducing the environmental footprint of transportation. Tackling the transport and mobility issue has a significant impact on other (socio-) economic and environmental aspects as well as on the quality of life and the wellbeing of the urban populations. In China and Europe alike multi-modal mobility systems and new mobility services are investigated to deal with problems of commuting and congestion. The European case study, the JPI UE project Smart Commuting, analysed mobility behaviour of commuters in three countries to identify the need for and potential of new mobility services. Results have not only been reflected with policy makers but are also translated into business solutions with transportation companies. The case of Shanghai illustrates how different smart services can enhance the multimodal transport behaviour where busses, cars, trains and bikes play an essential role. Through an innovative app solution, different transport modes are connected, and door-to-door travel planning is offered in a multi-modal way.

3. 2. Case Study in Europe

JPI UE: *Smart Commuting*

Smart Commuting started in 2016 to study new ways of combining work and life on the move with intelligent and sustainable transport system services. The project has studied commuter flows and contributed to the development of services for smarter traveling, striving to make commuting easier, more flexible and efficient, and lowering costs for travelers. In focus are three Travel-to-Work areas in Austria, Finland and Switzerland and how new types of mobility concepts could support people and cities.

The first objective was to identify the changing needs of mobile workers by collecting data by surveys, interviews and workshops. Smart Commuting has thereby been able to compare cultural and geographical contexts in three countries using an in-depth case study method. In this context, Smart Commuting examines how legislation, culture, and technology policies influence the adaptation of the chosen mobility solution. For example, cities have to address commuting when developing public services and assessing new infrastructure investments.

The second objective was to increase the sustainability of mobility with new mobility concepts and services. This was done by having the on-demand shared taxi service partners Kyyti in Finland and ISTmobil in Austria. The project helps to evaluate how these concepts meet the evolving needs of mobile workers and discover some common ground for service design and city planning policies. The Kyyti system for sharing taxis by the project partner Tuup Oy has partly been developed in the project.

"The project was designed so that project's research activities support implementations. The stakeholders did not have to wait for our final observations, and for example, we have been able to be agile and support our company partners already during the service development process" says Prof. Matti Vartiainen from the Aalto University who has been the project leader with Teemu Surakka being project manager.

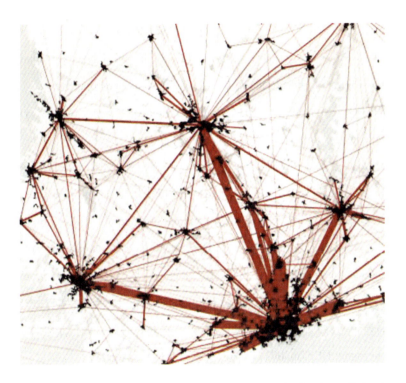

Figure 16   Commuting between population centers in Southern Finland
Soure: YKR, 2014, used under CC BY 4.0.

In Austria, ISTmobil GmbH, a provider of a shared taxi

system, gave the project's researchers access to the data about the use of their service to estimate the benefits of using such a system. Since different data sources exist with varying aggregation levels, accessibility and completeness, the identification of key aspects of mobility services was based on the incorporation of the mobility data from different sources. The analysis of the data provided possibilities to design more user-need-based services than before.

Over time the mobility of the workforce is increasing due to technology development, commuting and the nature of work. However, looking at the current situation, there is much more potential for the ISTmobil services with only 0.06 % of commuters from the district of Korneuburg to Vienna utilising the service. From our other cases, the Growth Corridor in Finland is a similar Travel-to-Work area near the capital city Helsinki that could benefit from ISTmobil or similar mobility solutions. During the project, the service was expanded to the surrounding municipalities of Graz with the name GUSTmobil.

"We took into account the institutional culture in each country. In Finland we are quite heavily focusing on enabling private companies to implement new services and to make technical innovations, whereas in the Swiss culture these new services are more strongly considered as only supplementing public transportation and the whole sector is pretty much in the hands of two federal companies", says Vartiainen. He goes on to say "One of our findings concerns the policy issues, what are the necessary

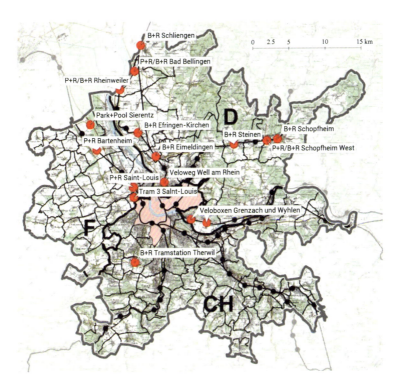

Figure 17   Mobility projects supported by the "Pendlerfonds"
Source: Canton of BaselStadt, 2016. Used with permission.

local policies in organizing these mobility services—to what extent are they scalable? The local context depends very much on the implementation of relevant policies. " The project has also pointed out differences between the countries concerning the governmental structure and the number of stakeholders involved in organizing transportation.

Ⅰ. Findings and next steps

The Smart Commuting project has collected statistics on mobile workers and their needs; for example, how many children they have, the number of cars they own, the number of motorcycles and e-bikes in the household, and they type of living environment they occupied. Results show, how much time the commuters spend travelling and the distance between the home and the workplace but also how they use the technical system and different applications, and what they are doing during their commute and what rationalities they have when choosing a certain mode of transport.

"I think we have generated all kinds of findings, but the most important, to some extent, is the user survey in the three countries comparing the mobility profiles and the mobility needs in each country and how the users perceive the suitability of new mobility solutions to their needs", says Vartiainen.

"We have gained a lot of insights for the transportation actors about the differences between the countries concerning what services are emerging and how they are used. We have been invited to discuss our findings in Urban Agenda for the EU policy labs, which shows there is a need for these insights and policy guidelines", says Teemu Surakka.

The project has generated new knowledge for the planning of commuter systems, services and city and region planning but also on what is important when setting up mobility systems and solutions. For the companies involved, this has meant not only the joint development of their services but also direct commercial effect as Tuup Oy has through the project started a co-operation with SwissPostBus.

"That was one of the drivers in joining the consortium. And now, we have been building a similar service to Kyyti in Switzerland. It has been in test use for a couple of months and will be launched in Brugg outside Zurich", says Johanna Taskinen from Tuup/Kyyti. Tuup Oy is also going to start a new project with a company customer to test their solution in an organizational setting in the City of Oulu. Ms. Taskinen sees the project as one part of the continuous product development.

The study also gave answers to the market potential of new mobility modes, such as car sharing, on-demand services and bike sharing and what a commuter would like to see as enablers, such as more space for a laptop, a better internet connection, quiet working spaces and the permission to work while traveling from the employer. The findings lay the foundation for the next project that is based on Smart Commuting.

"We have submitted a proposal for a Horizon 2020 call with more or less the same partners, but now adding city partners with their challenges in sustainable commuting. We have the evidence to step up to making the best possible policies and tools for cities to work, and this is the main takeaway. I am happy with the collaboration in the project", concludes Matti Vartiainen.

Smart Commuting: smart and mobile work in growth regions

Duration: 2016 – 2018

Internet: https://smartcommuting.eu/

Contact: Prof. Dr. Matti Vartiainen, Aalto University

E-mail: matti.vartiainen@aalto.fi

Partners: Aalto University, AIT Austrian Institute of Technology, tbw research GesmbH, ZHAW Zurich University of Applied Sciences, Virta Ltd. (Liikennevirta Oy), AC2SG Software Oy, Tuup Oy, ISTmobil GmbH, Growth Corridor Finland,

Office for Mobility of the Canton of Basel-Stadt

Acknowledgement: This project has received funding from the European Union's Horizon 2020 research and innovation programme under grant agreement No 646453

3. 3. **Case Study in China**

Urban public transport is a key component of sustainable urban development, as it offers a more energy efficient way for transport and mobility than the private automobile in general[1]. Thus, the public transit-oriented development contributes to carbon emission reduction and thus sustainable development compared to automobile-oriented development. Figure 18 is an example showing that, within peak hours, the bus or metro system consumes less energy and emits less greenhouse gases than the private automobile per passenger kilometer from a life-cycle perspective accounts for all emissions[2].

For traffic congestion alleviation, a number of cities in China have started to adopt travel demand measures (e. g. imposing

---

[1]   World Bank (2012) Sustainable Low-Carbon City Development in China.

[2]   Chester and Horvath, "Environmental Assessment of Passenger Transportation should Include Infrastructure and Supply Chains", *Environmental Researh Letters*, 4, 2009, pp. 1 – 8.

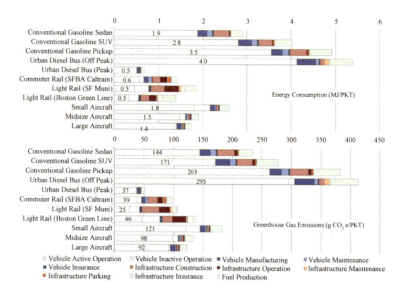

Figure 18   Life-Cycle Emissions by Passenger Kilometer

Notes: For energy consumption and GHG emissions per PKT, the vehicle operation components are shown with gray patterns; other vehicle components are shown in shades of blue; infrastructure components are shown in shades of red and orange; the fuel production component is shown in green; and all components appear in the order they are shown in the legend.

Source: Chester and Horvath, 2009.

restrictions on new car purchases and use and increased parking fees) from the lens of the travel demand perspective following the examples of Shanghai and Beijing[1]. The adoption of these measures together with the further development of the public transit system, such as the metro system and RBT (e. g. in Guangzhou), have contributed to the increase in the public transportation ridership and the reduction in the use of private vehicles. These, to some text, have reduced traffic congestion in those cities, although there may be still a long way to go to achieve significant reductions. The following is a good practice of smart transport and mobility in Shanghai Municipality.

3. 4. **Case Study: Smart Transport and Mobility in Shanghai Municipality**[2]

The development of smart transport and mobility in Shanghai has been accelerated after the Shanghai World Expo 2010. Since then, smart transportation technologies have been widely used in transport sectors, such as rail transit, buses and trolleybuses, public parking, transport hubs, which contributes greatly to

---

[1]   Wang, J. and He, D. , "Sustainable Urban Development in China: Challenges and Achievements, *Mifigation and Adaptation Strategies for Global Change*, 20, 2015, pp. 665 – 682.

[2]   http: //www. sohu. com/a/198740991 _ 182825; http: //www. shanghai. gov. cn/nw2/nw2314/nw2315/nw4411/u21aw1236157. html; http: //www. shanghai. gov. cn/nw2/nw2314/nw2315/nw4411/u21aw1283651. html.

transport management and information sharing with the public.

In order to provide a one-stop platform for transportation information, the Shanghai Municipal Transportation Commission released the Shanghai Transport App. The App contains 12 functional modules (see Figure 19), covering air, water and land

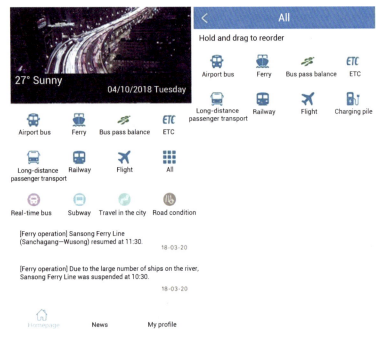

Figure 19   Shanghai Transport App

Source: Apple Store.

transport, i. e. real-time bus, metro, road condition, ferry, airport shuttle bus information, etc. It can help residents plan their door-to-door journeys on foot, by public transport and/or car. Residents can also check the balance of their Public Transport and ETC Cards and find information on the location of electric car charging points.

There are other popular transportation applications in Shanghai, such as Shanghai BusApp, and Shanghai Metro App, specializing in providing information on bus, express and highways, and metro services respectively. To realize the above-mentioned smart transport and mobility in Shanghai, there are strong hardware and software support and real-time data feeds. For instance, the data on the 648 bus routes in the municipality that can be accessed by the Shanghai Bus App. The Shanghai Ba-Shi Public Transportation (Group) calculates optimal bus departure and arrival times taking into consideration route planning, road conditions, bus locations to realize the intelligent scheduling system. So far, there are nearly 4,000 buses covering over 340 bus routes in Pudong District that have been integrated into the intelligent scheduling system.

The above mentioned public transport together with biking sharing in Shanghai have contributed tremendously to solving the "last mile" problem of getting peoplefrom public transport to their destinations through bikes. Figure 20 shows that 90% of the dockless shared bikes are used near bus stops and 51% of such bikes are used near metro stations in Shanghai in 2016[①]. It is worth

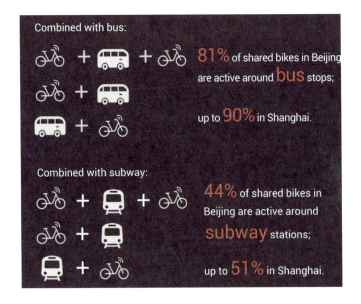

Figure 20　The Combined Usage of the Public Transport and the
Bike Sharing System in Shanghai and Beijing Municipalities in 2016

Source: Beijing Tsinghua Tongheng Urban Planning and Design Institute and Mobike, 2017 White Paper: Bike-sharing and the City, 2017.

---

① Beijing Tsinghua Tongheng Urban Planning and Design Institute and Mobike, the White Paper on Bike-Sharing and Urban Development 2017, 2017.

noting here that the data was collected from the area of 300 meters within bus stops and from the area of 500 meters within metro stations. There are some overlaps between the two area types. The case study of bike sharing will be illustrated separately in the next section.

4. Sharing Economy

4. 1. **Overview**

With the development of digital technologies, the sharing economy has become a reality. Combined with an upcoming tendency among urban populations towards sharing instead of owning, sharing services are influencing urban life socially, environmentally and economically. Sharing economy provides potential to challenge established routines. In Europe and China, new sharing schemes are significantly influencing urban life, consumption patterns and have the potential to significantly contribute to sustainable urban development. The JPI UE project E4 – share developed models for flexible, efficient and economic viable electric car-sharing systems. In the project, different car-sharing models were compared, user incentives determined, and supporting policy frameworks investigated using the case of the City of Vienna. In China, the sharing economy has seen significant growth recently. New sharing schemes and business models have created a boom of Bike Sharing since 2015. Today, bike sharing is especially relevant for "the last mile", the distance between public transportation and people's final destination.

4. 2. Case Study in Europe

JPI UE project: E4 – share

The E4 – share project lays the foundation for flexible, efficient and economically viable car-sharing systems based on electric cars which allows citizens to efficiently use and shift between different modes of transport. The objective of the project was to develop generic models for electric car-sharing systems that can be applied in cities around Europe and to study and solve the optimization problems which arise in their design and operations.

There is a growing concern regarding the problems related to unsustainable transportation systems in cities, including congestions, air pollution and noise, and how it affects citizens' health and life quality. Cities are confronted with severe challenges and need to manage a transformation process that will lead to less pollution and less energy and land consumption, while increasing the quality of public space available to citizens. Optimizing the transport system in cities is one central task which would improve urban mobility systems.

Car-sharing is part of the so called "sharing economy" (The Economist, 2013) which means the sharing of goods and services respectively, such as renting instead of owning a car. Users have the choice between small and large cars, fuel-driven or electric cars as well as free-floating and station-based cars. Car-sharing systems are becoming more and more popular and the number of operating companies has increased all over the world in the last few years. On the other hand, some operators have already withdrawn from the market, indicating a lack of sustainable business models. In relation to the thematic area of sharing economy and the contribution of private sectors the project therefore gives valuable insights into the operators' user incentives and provides tools for optimizing technology and business models in an emergent market.

E4 – share is an international research project that was funded through the JPI Urban Europe pilot call II offering "models for ecological, economical, efficient and electric car-sharing". The project ended in 2017 and was led by the University of Vienna, AIT, tbw research (a non-profit organization engaged in research and innovation projects), Université Libre de Bruxelles and the University of Bologna in collaboration with car-sharing-operators.

Ⅰ. Vienna case study

The city of Vienna was used as a case study. The city was divided into different operating areas and the assumption of the demand was based on taxi data. Additional inputs included a fixed

Figure 21　A heat-map of the electric car sharing system

Notes: The darker colors indicate the more frequently used road segments (AIT—Austrian Institute of Technology).

investment budget for the car-sharing operator and a maximum walking distance of five minutes for car-sharing users. The aim of the model for Vienna was to optimize the expected sales as well as the locations and incentives as well as to model a balanced number of vehicles and stations.

The methods developed for modeling, optimization and simulation in the Vienna case are transferable and scalable and thus applicable to other cities and applications (for example, bike sharing, charging stations in public spaces).

There are basically two types of car-sharing services—station-based services where cars are being picked up and left by the user at fixed places in the city and free-floating services where cars are parked mostly anywhere in the city. The trend is towards free-floating services which are the ones most preferred by users. The mathematic models which have been developed in the project are applicable to both of the car-sharing services and the project had to answer many questions. For station-based systems questions like: Where do the stations have to be built? How many charging points per station make sense? Which customers can be served? All of these questions have been addressed. On the other hand, free-floating systems not only need an efficient distribution of charging stations, but also an incentive strategy or incentive systems to make maintenance, charging of vehicles and other necessary maintenance work as efficient as possible.

Ⅱ. Insights into user incentives

The project has gained insights into what incentives are effective to reduce fleet management efforts and provide new ways for car-sharing companies to optimize operations.

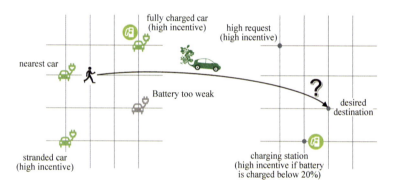

Figure 22   User incentives

For the analysis of existing, and especially potential future incentives, as well as possible management tasks that can be taken over by users, a detailed research of existing car-sharing companies as well as workshops and an online survey were carried out. Various factors such as income, car-sharing usage behavior, interest in possible incentives and their amount were related to each other. The results were integrated into the mathematical models and presented in a *User incentives catalogue.*

Ⅲ. Solution examples for car-sharing operators

The project E4 – share provides example solutions for the car-sharing location planning and charging stations as well as numerous evaluations and analyzes on e. g. vehicle usage intensity, pick-up and return of vehicles in the system or modeled performance of the system with different size of the operating area. These solutions can be a useful decision support for solving the operators' key strategic, tactical and operational problems. Offering electric cars instead of fuel driven ones offers chances of improving urban quality of life but of course poses specific challenges for both service providers and city administrations.

The models developed based on the Vienna case are generally applicable for optimized planning and operation at various planning levels. Simulations based on these complex mathematical models and an abstracted network with simplified representations of stations, customer requests and walking ranges are available on the project website①.

IV. Identified opportunities for urban decisions makers

The outcomes of the project provide arguments for a regulated market to take better advantage of technological solutions and realize efficient and sustainable urban systems and networks.

"At present the city of Vienna does not regulate the car-sharing market and operators", says Marlene Hawelka, project leader at tbw research, "but shared mobility services can be a valuable asset for urban mobility acting as a supplement to public transport and can help to reduce the land consumption of the mobility system. Therefore, a more widespread car-sharing system is needed where citizens in the outer city districts also could access the system. In today's non-regulated market the car-sharing companies operate mostly in the central districts where you can also easily walk and take the tram. "

In addition, digital platforms and MaaS (Mobility as a Service) can help to seamlessly integrate new services into the existing urban transport system.

---

① http: //www. univie. ac. at/e4 − share/.

E4 – share: Models for ecological, economical, efficient, electric car-sharing

Duration: 2014 – 2017

Internet: www. univie. ac. at/e4 – share

Contact: Markus Leitner, University of Vienna

E-mail: markus. leitner@ univie. ac. at

Partners: AIT Austrian Institute of Technology, Université Libre de Bruxelles, University of Bologna, tbw research GesmbH, University of Vienna

---

4. 3. Case Study in China

The rapid development of the sharing economy in the past decade is the result of the pursuit of better value redistribution and collaborative consumption and the growing salience of natural resource constraints after the international financial crisis[1]. The peer-to-peer (P2P) sharing of access to under-utilized goods and services online has contributed to the reduction of ecological

---

[1]   https: //www. ted. com/talks/lisa_ gansky_ the_ future_ of_ business_ is_ the_ mesh; https: //www. youtube. com/watch? v = AQa3kUJPEko; Schor, J. and Fitzmaurice, C. , " Collaborating and Connecting: The Emergence of the Sharing Economy" , in *Handbook on Research on Sustainable Consumption* , eds. , Lucia Reisch and John Thogersen, 2015, Cheltenham, UK: Edward Elgar; McLaren, D. and Agyeman, J. , *Sharing Cities: A Case for Truly Smart and Sustainable Cities*, 2015, Cambridge, Massachusetts: The MIT Press.

footprint[1]. Thus, the sharing economy has the potential to offer a new pathway to achieve sustainability[2].

The world has witnessed a sharing economy boom in recent years. So does the sharing economy in China[3]. The term of sharing economy was defined as "the total sum of economic activities with the main feature of usage sharing that is achieved by mobilizing massive but scattered resources to meet diverse requirements through the use of modern information technologies such as the Internet" in the *Annual Report on the Development of Sharing Economy in China* (2017) released by the Sharing Economy Research Center of the State Information Center. The trading volume of the sharing economy in China was 4. 9205 trillion yuan in 2017 according to the *Annual Report on the Development of Sharing Economy in China* (2018)[4], which increased by 47. 2% over the last year. Over 700 million people were involved in the sharing

---

[1]   Cheng, M. , "Sharing Economy: A Review and Agenda for Future Research", *International Journal of Hospitality Management*, 57, 2016, pp. 60 – 70.

[2]   Heinrichs, H. , "Sharing Economy: A Potential New Pathway to Sustainability", *Gaia*, 22 (4), 2013, pp. 228 – 231.

[3]   Wen, S. , "Research on Innovation in Holistic Governance for A More Effective System of Urban Bike Sharing Supervision", *E-Government*, 04, 2018, pp. 21 – 31.

[4]   http: //tech. ifeng. com/a/20180228/44890942_ 0. shtml; http: //baijiahao. baidu. com/s? id = 1594089458520055061&wfr = spider&for = pc.

economy, an increase by about 100 million compared to the last year's figure.

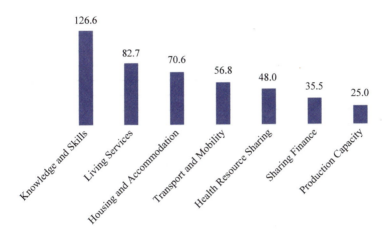

Figure 23   The Trade Volume Growth in the Sharing

Economy by Sector in China in 2017

Source: Reproduced based on the data from the Annual Report on the Development of Sharing Economy in China, 2018.

Figure 23 shows the trade volume growth in the sharing economy by sector in China in 2017, with the growth rates of the Knowledge and Skills sector (126. 6%), the Living Services section (82. 7%) and the Housing and Accommodation sector (70. 6%) among the top three out of the seven key sectors. It is estimated that the average annual growth rate of the sharing economy would maintain above 30% in the next five years.

The rapid development of the sharing economy may be not directly linked to the low-carbon development of cities in China. It may depend on the nature of the sectors and how they are related to the reduction in ecological footprint. For instance, bike and car sharing in the Transport and Mobility sector contributes to reducing the level of automobile use, thus having positive impacts on low-carbon and sustainable development. However, some services delivering over-packaged goods in the Living Services sector may not be the case. The following is case study of bike sharing in China. Admittedly, bike sharing may have potential problems, such as financial sustainability and urban management. The focus of this case study will be on the relationship between bike sharing and sustainable urban development in the Chinese context.

4. 4. Case Study: Bike Sharing in China

There is a bike-sharing boom in China in recent years, which is enabled by digital innovations. The aim of bike sharing is to solve the "last mile" problem of getting people from public transport to their destinations through bikes as mentioned in the previous section. Bike sharing is a new business model of the sharing economy in which companies collaborate with local governments to offer bike rental services in or around places, such as public spaces, residential areas, business districts, bus stops and metro stations[1].

Bike sharing is also a recent development of public bicycle sharing in China. There are two phases of development with the advance of innovative technologies. The first phase started around 2008 when the concept of public bicycle was introduced to the Chinese market, with shared bikes and docking stations. Hangzhou Public Bicycle is a good example of public bicycle sharing in China. In 2008, the Hangzhou city government launched the Hangzhou Public Bicycle programas a seamless feeder service to public transit throughout the city in light of growing traffic congestion and environmental concerns. The program initially started with 2, 800 bicycles, 30 fixed docking stations and 30 mobile docking stations (movable to meet demand) (see Figure 24)[2]. As of January 5, 2013, it had become the largest public

---

① Wen, S. , "Research on Innovation in Holistic Governance for A More Effective System of Urban Bike Sharing Supervision", *E-Government*, 04, 2018, pp. 21 – 31.

② Shaheen, S. , Zhang, H. , Martin, E. and Guzman, S. , *Transportation Research Record: Journal of the Transportation Research Board*, 2247, 2011, pp. 33 – 41.

bicycle sharing system in the world, with 66, 500 bicycles operating from 2, 700 stations, which contributed tremendously to the reduction of carbon emissions in the city[1].

Figure 24　Hangzhou Public Bicycle

Source: http://policytransfer.metropolis.org/case-studies/hangzhou-china-urban-public-bicycle-sharing-program.

The dock-less bike sharing in China has seen a rapid expansion since 2015 with the development of innovative technologies. There are furious competitions between the bike sharing and the public bicycle sharing, and between bike sharing

---

① https://web.archive.org/web/20140808045713/; http://www.zj.xinhuanet.com/newscenter/focus/2013 –01/05/c_ 114258328. htm.

startups in China. Among many bike-sharing startups, Mobike and OfO enjoy the largest market shares currently. The dockless bikes are equipped with GPS and other innovative technologies, which collect big data from bike usage to help achieve intelligent scheduling through improved optimization algorithms[1].

The bike-sharing boom provides residents with a "smart" alternative for short urban journeys, which is conducive to low-carbon and sustainable urban development. According to *the 2017 White Paper: Bike-sharing and the City*[2] published by Beijing Tsinghua Tongheng Urban Planning and Design Institute and Mobike, the proportion of bike rides in the most popular modes of urban transport (i. e. cars, buses, the metro and bike rides) had increased by 6. 1% (from 5. 5% to 11. 6%) in 2016 since the introduction of bike sharing in 2015. The total distance of the nation-wide bike ride had reached 2. 5 billion kilometers, which contributed to reducing 540 thousand tons of carbon emissions (Figure 25). Bike sharing, to some extent, had reduced car

① Wen, S. (2018) Research on Innovation in Holistic Governance for A More Effective System of Urban Bike Sharing Supervision, *E-Government*, 04, pp. 21 – 31.

② http: //www. fietsberaad. nl/? lang = en&repository = White + paper + 2017 + Bike-sharing + and + the + City.

dependency, with the proportion of journeys by car in the most popular modes of urban transport decreased by 3.2% (from 29.8% to 26.6%) over the same period of time.

Figure 25   Bike Sharing Changes Urban Mobility and
Contributes to Reducing Carbon Emissions

Source: Beijing Tsinghua Tongheng Urban Planning and Design Institute and Mobike, 2017 White Paper: Bike-sharing and the City, 2017.

5. Smart Urban Governance

5.1. Overview

To effectively implement and design strategies for sustainable urban development, new collaborative governance processes involving private and public stakeholders are called for. Enabling technologies, big data and "real time" action offer new ways for innovative and smart urban governance and management. Multiple information sources are nowadays easily available for urban decision making, while appropriate tools and methods are required to consolidate and synthesise them. The JPI UE project, UrbanData2Decide, processed information from public social media and open data libraries to develop a decision support system for urban governance. At the same time digital technologies and social media support participatory planning and governance. Another JPI UE project Incubators for Public Space embedded such new technologies in participatory planning processes to allow all stakeholders to contribute to urban planning. The project implemented Urban Living Labs in London, Brussels and Turin. In China, e-governance services are implemented in many cities. 80 Chinese cities have been involved in "Information-for-the Public" pilot projects, which aim to set up online e-governance service platforms. The Smart Urban Governance approach of Weihai City aimed at tapping the potential of smart technologies by fostering institutional change, capacity building in public administration and socio-technological innovations.

5. 2. Case Studies in Europe

JPI UE Project : UrbanData2Decide

The UrbanData2Decide project aims to extract and process information from two sources, public social media and open data libraries. The aim is to develop new methods to combine existing big data pools and expert knowledge into one optimal framework to support holistic decision making for urban management.

Every day, hundreds of decisions are taken in a municipality. These days, urban decision makers are faced with both unprecedented challenges as well as new opportunities as the environment around them grows ever more complex. However, sources with the potential to be important to decision-making have so far remained largely untapped. UrbanData2Decide provides answers utilizing the increasing amount of data.

UrbanData2Decide started in 2014① and seeks to create the tools needed to react to and make decisions in the digital age. The extracted and processed information from social media and open

---

① http: //www. urbandata2decide. eu/wp-content/uploads/deliverables/Urban Data2Decide-D1. 1-Kick-off-Meeting-Report. pdf.

data sources combined with advice from expert panels, is used to support local governments in their move towards a holistic, sustainable and well-founded decision-making process which considers the views and perspectives of all relevant stakeholders. The challenges include gaining a better control of data, broadening the data available and creating more awareness regarding positive effects of open data and other data sources. In practice this is done by gathering the data, analyzing it and then visualizing it. The case study conducted in the city of Vienna presents ten examples on how the UrbanData2Decide decision support tool could be leveraged in ongoing and future projects.

Ⅰ. The structure of UrbanData2Decide

The project is in the context part divided into three sub groups: domain, stakeholder and spatial level, raising among other things data ethics, the data needed and the access type. In the visualizing a spectrum of different ways of showing the data in an easy and understandable way has been created. The last part of UrbanData2Decide is the key target of decision making: the actors, the method, involvement of experts and the technical solutions for that but also frequency, level and the duration are elements in the process.

We can see a move towards the use of "data science" in city contexts as a way of informing decisions, and I think our research fits into this trend. "The ideal outcome is that we get better data to policymakers which allows them to make better decisions" says Dr Jonathan Bright, Senior Research Fellow at the Oxford Internet Institute at the University of Oxford.

The project leader, SYNYO specializes in researching and engineering novel ICT-based solutions applied to data analytics and information visualization. The focus of SYNYO was situational awareness, what is happening in a certain city and solutions for problems encountered were investigated, and some of them were selected for development: trend monitor (i. e. text-based analysis of social media and online media such as newspapers, blogs), a visual monitor (images, videos), organisations' streams (social streams), and open data maps. The University of Copenhagen focused on images and in particular those from Instagram.

The City of Copenhagen took part in the project as part of the city's aim of trying to make data available to the public in order to make the citizens better informed, and to enable dialogue. The case study conducted in the city of Copenhagen focuses on municipal spatial planning, including information on how decisions are made

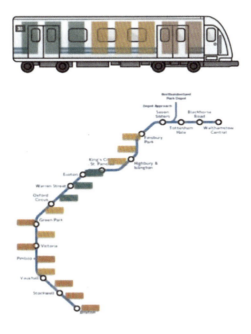

Figure 26　London Underground Crowding Indicators

for a longer period in collaboration with the citizens.

Another example on how these kinds of urban data can be used are the train signal data demonstrator for the London Underground (goingunderground. herokuapp. com) by the Open Data Institute. Signal graphs visualize the development of train data over time and allow comparison between multiple sensor data sets. The data is the base for the visualization of train carriage occupancy levels for

upcoming trains at specific stations at specific times for the Victoria
Line.

Figure 27   Vision of integrated data visualisation and

decision-making solutions to forecast and manage

complex urban challenges

II. UrbanDataVisualiser and UrbanDecisionMaker[1]

Building on the broad data collections in the form of social
media content and open data sets, the UrbanDataVisualiser
aggregates, structures and visualises this data using a multi-layered
and multi-dimensional approach. The framework extensively uses
data mining, sentiment analysis and visualisation techniques and
leads to the development of a proof-of-concept demonstrator to

[1]   http://www. urbandata2decide. eu/wp-content/uploads/deliverables/Urban
Data2Decide-D3. 1-UrbanDataVisualiser-Report. pdf.

showcase the information using intuitive and clear dashboards. For the development of the UrbanDataVisualiser a report on different tools in the countries was written, showcasing different ways of monitoring and visualizing data and the use of different data sources, and making an overview over the tools and the sources used. Here the project also gives an overview over the different data types and the accessibility of each of them[1]. The Open Data Institute developed the visualization tools and examples.

They developed different ways and methods to visualize, which you could use yourself, "you could see how you can do it with different forms of visualizations in order to make it easier to understand the great amount of data" says Per-Olof Hallin, Malmö University and one of the project participants.

The tool UrbanDecisionMaker on the other hand integrates external experts and advisors using scientific multi-round expert integration methods and tools such as the Delphi method, a structured communication technique, developed as a systematic, interactive forecasting method which relies on a panel of experts. It

---

① http: //www. urbandata2decide. eu/wp-content/uploads/deliverables/Urban Data2Decide-D3. 1-UrbanDataVisualiser-Report. pdf.

features among other things the tools Expert Integrator, Collective Deliberation Tool and Expert Pool[1].

The result of UrbanData2Decide shows the need to develop visualization tools and the project has been able to test several prototypes. Results from these tests have been used in projects such as urban safety and security.

The result in our case was that data is not being used, there is no policy on how to work around it and there are no good methods. "This is partly because people are not used to working with these kind of data sources and there many different actors" says Per-Olof Hallin.

We are in an experimental phase where lots of cities are trying lots of different things with data, and my recommendation would be to be open to this type of experimentation at an institutional level: allow your staff to work with data, get access to it, play around, and try and develop useful tools. "This kind of 'start-up' culture has historically been very difficult to develop in a local government context (at least in the UK) where budgets are very strained and

---

[1]　http://www. urbandata2decide. eu/wp-content/uploads/deliverables/Urban Data2Decide-D3. 3-Interface-Design. pdf.

there is a high fear of failure" comments Jonathan Bright regarding recommendations for others.

UrbanData2Decide has served as an inspiration for other projects when developing methods for data collecting and sharing, for example, in the making of joint overviews over situations between different stakeholders such as public offices and private companies, for example city councils and property owners. UrbanData2Decide has been instrumental in creating processes for teaching and the development of shared views regarding data as part of developing cities.

UrbanData2Decide: Integrated data visualisation and decision making solutions to forecast and manage complex urban challenges

Duration: 2014 – 2016

Internet: www. urbandata2decide. eu

Contact: Peter Leitner

E-mail: peter. leitner@ synyo. com

Partners: University of Oxford, Oxford Internet Institute, Malmö University, Open Data Institute, IT University of Copenhagen, Software Development Group, ZSI Centre for Social Innovation, SYNYO GmbH, Research and Development Department

---

JPI UE Project: Incubators of public space

The Incubators of public spaces is a project that provides tools and means to enhance active involvement from local stakeholders in activities which seek to shape their local environments. Incubators addresses ways to harness the power of new technological possibilities and integrate them within co-creative urban planning and governance, which includes a plurality of stakeholders in the making of vibrant public spaces. Incubators of public spaces allows local stakeholders to go online or join a public meeting, and easily shape their own scenarios for their local area, with clear and simple 3D models of spaces. They can stroll around or freely fly through their environment and transform their surroundings, exploring and making changes. Then, crowdfunding is the scenario to provide their support.

Ⅰ. Embedding new technology in participatory planning processes

New developments in technology from Artificial Intelligence (AI) to online web interfaces, "dashboards" of urban performance and visualizations of development proposals, have unleashed great potential for users of the built environment to play a more active role in interpreting and proactively shaping their built environments. These developments not only pose technological challenges—in terms of design and management of human-computer interactions—

but also raise questions of how those technological challenges are bound up with the aptitudes and inclinations of different kinds of user. Hence, they raise questions such as "who is best able to make the most use of these technological processes?", and "how best they may be embedded in specific participatory planning processes?".

II. Online platforms and scenarios

Incubators is an ambitious international research project funded in JPI Urban Europe's second pilot call (2014 – 2017) led by Politecnico di Torino in cooperation with Innovation Service Network GmbH (ISN), Katholieke Universiteit Leuven, Neurovation GmbH, University College London and the City of Torino.

Incubators aims to support the self-organisation of places and communities, enhancing the factors that motivate, encourage and enable urban actors to reach a common understanding. This will create space for coordinating actions by reasoned argument, consensus, and cooperation rather than simply relying on top down strategic thinking. The means to this goal are information and communication technologies which empowers actors to advance their co-creation capabilities of urban space.

For this purpose, the project developed and applied an online

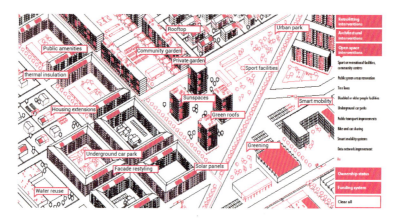

Figure 28　Example of a scenario generated in one
of the case studies

platform. The online platform allows public users to access information about the site, and to remotely and interactively make innovative proposals for interventions in the urban fabric (for example, adding anything from a bench to a whole park; or in principle, moving existing elements around) all visualized in 3D scenarios. Scenarios present a coherent overview of the interventions of various scales and budgets that can be flexibly bespoke and implemented on demand, giving the community the capability to control its own progress and "mold" its own place.

An important part of the project was to develop a system—a taxonomy—to transfer conceptually the knowledge about the domain of urban space into a hierarchical and interrelated semantic structure with relevant concepts, elements and their mutual relationships, providing explicit and unambiguous definitions.

Ⅲ. Crowdsourcing ideas and crowdfunding projects

Open innovation and crowd technologies were another feature of the project. In the last few years crowdfunding has become a promising tool for generating funds not only for private projects, public organisations or start-ups, but also for urban areas. Besides the acquisition of financial resources, crowd-related activities offer several added values regarding innovation aspects and risk management.

The project has implemented a software platform for crowdsourced and crowdfunded placemaking that allows the crowd to be activated throughout the whole innovation process (see Figure 29), crowdsourcing ideas by inviting a wide target group to submit their ideas in response to a defined challenge, to provide feedback on project ideas, or to vote for the best ones. Ideas that have been evaluated successfully in the first phase are further supported for promotion on an appropriate crowdfunding platform. Thus, the realisation of a collaboratively developed new project is supported by the crowd both by gathering the relevant know-how and raising funds.

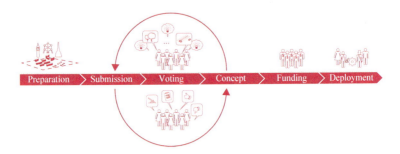

Figure 29   Overview of the Crowd Creativity and
Crowdfunding Process

Ⅳ. Urban Living Labs in London, Brussels and Turin

The project's methodology and technology has been tested in
urban living labs in three cities. Each living lab had the opportunity
to unfold in its own particular and context-based configuration that
could best support the local self-organisation of places.

The London case study is focused on an existing 14 hectare
housing estate, the Pollards Hill. The Brussels living lab is located
at the Josaphat site, consisting of a 30 hectare large area currently
planned to be transformed into a new sustainable neighbourhood.
The Josaphat site, as such, forms an interesting case for
experimentation on how the Incubator tool can support the current

and future uses of Josaphat and the inclusion of the aspirations of the citizens as well as the public stakeholders.

The Turin living lab is focused on the regeneration of Quartiere Mirafiori Sud a social housing neighbourhood of high-rise apartment buildings built in the mid-sixties which totals about 2700 dwellings and 6000 inhabitants. Through design workshops and other living lab activities local stakeholders have been engaged in the definition of collaboration and self-organisation scenarios for the rehabilitation of public spaces and buildings.

V. The digital platform is ready for implementation

Experiences with the Incubators methodology in the Brussels, London and Turin cases have been promising. "It seems the taxonomy triggers discussions and helps explicating ideas. Allowing stakeholders to shape their own scenarios in 3D models proves to be a promising approach that enhances the understanding among lay people and thereby their capability to contribute to the shaping of their local communities," says Luca Cancparo, Researcher at Politecnico di Torino, Italy. Luca Caneparo continues by saying "Testing the design platform and the taxonomy of objects has brought insights in the variance in how stakeholders understand objects in a map. There are differences across countries which implies that the tool needs to be tailored and adapted to different countries".

The digital platform is in principle ready to be scaled up from the pilot cases and to be employed in other projects at a neighbourhood level, however legal property rights are a barrier for wider spread of the tool at the moment.

Incubators of public spaces

Duration: 2014 – 2017

Internet: www. jpi-urbaneurope. eu/incubators

Contact: Luca Caneparo, Politecnico di Torino

E-mail: luca. caneparo@ polito. it

Partners: Innovation Service Network GmbH (ISN), Katholieke Universiteit Leuven, Neurovation GmbH, University College London, City of Torino, Politecnico di Torino

---

5. 3. Case Study in China

Similar to the concept of smart city, fragmentation exists in the concept of smart city governance. But it is widely agreed that smart city governance is not merely a technological issue, as technologies themselves are not likely to make a city smarter; fostering a smart city requires a political understanding of the technologies. Thus, smart urban governance is rather a complex process with institutional change and the acknowledgment of socio-technical governance and about creating new forms of human collaboration by using ICTs to achieve better outcomes and more open governance[1]. The synergy between social structure and new technologies has been the focus of e-government research over the past decades, with a special emphasis on investigating how new technologies could be used to improve the quality and effectiveness of government[2].

In China, progress and institutional breakthroughs have been made in smart urban governance in the past few years, with the application of more advanced information and network technology. "Internet + " has transformed urban management model and service provision and delivery models in a profound way. Smarter ways to manage population and monitor urban road networks and the smart emergency response system are among the typical examples of smart urban governance.

So far, 80 cities have carried out the "Information-for-the Public" pilot projects. The e-governance has increased government

---

[1]   Meijer, A. and Bolívar, M. ,   "Governing the Smart City: A Review of the Literature on Smart Urban Governance", *International Review of Administrative Sciences*, 82 (2) , 2016, pp. 392 –408.

[2]   Gil-Garcia R. , *Enacting Electronic Government Success: An Integrative Study of Government-wide Websites, Organizational Capabilities, and Institutions*, 2012, New York: Springer.

efficiency. The online service platforms introduced in Shandong, Zhejiang and Guangdong provinces have helped innovate and improve government services and transparency and law enforcement supervision in those cities.

5. 4. **Case Study: Smart Urban Governance in Weihai City**[①]

Weihai City set four major objectives when it started on its smart journey in 2013, three of which are closely related to smart urban governance, i. e. improving information infrastructure, enhancing governance capacity and providing, and managing public services in a more efficient way to improve people's livelihoods (the fourth one is stimulating urban economic development). The city has implemented various projects since then. The following are main focuses and achievements that are relevant to smart city governance.

(a) Integrating Departmental Resources to Realize E-governance

The city has invested 13. 5 million Yuan in a cloud-based e-governance system, installed 98 fiber optic links and integrated over 150 computer cluster and server devices in its governmental

---

① http: //www. wheitc. gov. cn/art/2018/3/14/art_ 6864_ 1163457. html.

departments. It has achieved uniform technical platform, computing and storage, integrated internal and external networks, and uniform security protection, and operation and maintenance in over 200 governmental departments.

(b) Improving Governance and Public Service Delivery through E-government

An integrated online system has been established in the city to improve the effectiveness and efficiency of its governance and public service delivery. The system includes a web portal for public service provision and information sharing[1], which can be accessed by citizens via PC, mobile phone, pad and digital TV; and multi-application citizen cards, by using which citizens can access smart community, healthcare, education, transport and mobility, tourism and cultural services.

(c) Introducing Smart Traffic Management to Reduce Congestion

The city has established a smart management and control platform and eight application systems to real-time monitor road traffic, integrating weather and other related data, automatically recognize key vehicles and report, and release traffic information on

---

[1]　http://www.whsmwy.com/wh_portal/.

major road junctions every 5 minutes. This has reduced the average waiting times during morning and evening peak hours of workdays in central districts of the city.

(d) Establishing the Smart Urban Construction Profile

The Profile includes an underground pipeline information system, urban construction filing system, onsite surveying data collection and project data collection system. It contains 967 files of 73 construction projects, covering 13, 994 – kilometer pipeline data of 96 Gigabits, covering six vertical sectors such as water supply, sewerage, gas, heating, electricity and telecommunications.

(e) Realizing Smart Water, Heat and Power Supply Management

The city has established a digitized water supply pipeline platform as well as water supply and sewerage coordination system to share information with other pipelines such as thermoelectricity, telecommunications and gas, and to realize onsite data real-time collection, automatic alarming and emergency coordination. Besides, it has established a smart power supply platform, realizing automatic collection of electricity usage data and automatic calculation of the electricity bills of 1. 31 million clients; and established an integrated smart power supply service system, consisting of the photovoltaics micro-grid energy storage system, light guide illumination system, energy saving lamps, smart power utilization service system, electric vehicle charging piles and energy efficiency services for residents. Furthermore, the city has established a smart heating management platform by upgrading 12,880 electric control valves in corridors of buildings and installing 330,000 indoor temperature control valves. This has reduced energy consumption by 27.6%, achieving the digitalization of heat metering, smartness of energy saving minoring and grid-based government supervision.

Chapter Four

Conclusions

The Conclusions section is intended to identify potential areas and ways of collaboration between Europe and China in sustainable urban development by analysing similarities and differences based on the good practices that are presented in this report. The good practices are selective rather than exhaustive, which represent, to some extent, related projects that have been funded by JPI UE and represent the sustainable urban development landscape in China.

The similarities in sustainable urban development between Europe and China are largely due to common urban challenges that both sides are facing. The differences are caused by different levels of urbanization, stages of socio-economic development as well as different approaches to governance and sustainable urban development between the two sides in general. The following two main differences can be determined from the cases investigated.

First, *Different Scales and Ways to Scale up.* In general, the European side has implemented more sustainable urban development projects in European cities on the project scale, which focuses on testing frameworks, approaches and/or innovative technologies and on the rollout of the already tested and approved demonstration projects. While the Chinese side has made more efforts on the city scale, which puts more emphasis on implementing projects concerning sustainable urban development in pilot cities and selecting and involving more eligible cities to start related projects.

Second, *Different Ways to Engage the Public.* Different ways have been witnessed on both sides in pubic engagement. According to the cases reflected in the report participatory approaches and co-creation methods are more strongly applied in European projects than the projects in Chinese cities. This may be due to the different governance approaches, a more top-down approach in Chinese cities, compared to a mixed model of top-down and bottom-up approaches in European cities.

Besides those differences in scale and policy and governance approaches the cases very well demonstrate that urban transitions requires integrated approaches and the involvement of different actors and stakeholders. In principle the following three main elements are key for driving sustainable urban development: (1) Availability of new technological solutions or social innovations that help to tackle a specific urban challenge. (2) New governance models as well as capacities and expertise in public administration fit to take highest advantage of such new technological and social opportunities and to create frameworks for urban transitions. (3) Mobilisation of citizens to create awareness of new approaches and solutions, drive behaviour change and support uptake of new solutions through early involvement in urban planning and local development.

According to this, efforts are needed on all scales and of all stakeholder groups to achieve sustainable urban development and research and innovation can strongly support these. To deal with this complexity, experimental settings on local or city level can help addressing specific challenges, through local pilot projects or living labs, allowing all stakeholders to cooperate, co-create, engage in urban development actions. Through this evidence can be created for good practice and conclusions can be drawn for wider implementation, including new policies, partnerships or business models. The examples given in the report highlight the potential of such multi-stakeholder approaches and create interesting references for further exchange between European and Chinese actors.

As sustainable urban development is a complex, long-term process, no single stakeholder can achieve the goal alone. Rather, it requires the collaboration between various stakeholders, such as cities, businesses, universities/research institutes and financial institutions. As the two sides are different in the above-mentioned aspects, it could be worth exploring each other's market by better understanding local knowledge and needs.

In general, the Europe side could provide Chinese cities with sustainable urban development framework and experiences (in related areas such as open data and urban living labs) by sharing its already tested and approved demonstration projects in collaboration with Chinese key stakeholders.

China has a huge market with enabling environment for innovation and could provide information and network technologies and physical infrastructure construction in European cities where needed in collaboration with European key stakeholders.

Partnerships may be needed to mobilize and integrate resources from the key stakeholders on both sides.

Given the fields of action and work of JPI UE and CCUD in Europe and China mentioned earlier, it could be helpful for the two organisations to play a facilitator role on each side. Suggested ways of cooperation may include, but not be limited to the following: conducting cooperative projects involving key stakeholders from both sides, with European and Chinese cities as demonstrator and/or observer cities; and organising events to gather expertise of European and Chinese experts and key stakeholders to better understand local knowledge as well as exchange ideas and experiences that could be transferable and adapt to other local contexts.